(Continued)

Building
Family Literacy
in an Urban
Community

Ruth D. Handel

TEACHERS
COLLEGE
PRESS

Teachers College, Columbia University
New York and London

Published by Teachers College Press, 1234 Amsterdam Avenue, New York, NY 10027

Library of Congress Cataloging-in-Publication Data

Handel, Ruth D.
  Building family literacy in an urban community / Ruth D. Handel.
      p.   cm. — (Language and literacy series)
  Includes bibliographical references (p.   ) and index.
  ISBN 0-8077-3895-6 (cloth : alk. paper). — ISBN 0-8077-3894-8
  (pbk. : alk. paper)
    1. Family literacy programs—New Jersey—Newark Case studies.
  2. Education, Urban—New Jersey—Newark Case studies.   I. Title.
  II. Series: Language and literacy series (New York, N.Y.)
  LC152.N58H36   1999
  302.2'244'0974932—dc21   99-39473

ISBN 0-8077-3894-8 (paper)
ISBN 0-8077-3895-6 (cloth)

Printed on acid-free paper
Manufactured in the United States of America

06 05 04 03 02 01 00 99   8 7 6 5 4 3 2 1

For Gerry

Contents

Acknowledgments

MANY PEOPLE CONTRIBUTED to this book. My primary debt of gratitude goes to the teachers and parents who let me share their work and lives during its preparation. I am grateful also to Montclair State University for a sabbatical leave, for released time under the Faculty Scholarship Incentive Program, and for a grant from the Montclair State University Alumni Association, all of which enabled me to conduct the interviews and other research.

Dawn Boyer's editorial comments on the first draft showed the way to improve the manuscript.

I wish also to thank Ellen Goldsmith for our years of conversations about family literacy. Ellen, whose insights are matched only by her generosity of spirit, read the manuscript and offered helpful suggestions. Meta Potts, former training director of the National Center for Family Literacy, and Rachele Ackerman, director of the Hackensack, New Jersey, Even Start program, provided important information about their organizations. Nancy Ares, Ruth Hayden, Cathy Lindsley, Rick Luderman, Susan Perkins, Meta Potts, Don Seaman, and Peggy Sissel, colleagues in the virtual community of the National Literacy Advocacy Listserve, and Linda Labbo, Barbara P. Laster, Lauren Leslie, Leslie Morrow, Laurie Elish-Piper, and Rose-Marie Weber of the National Reading Conference provided thoughtful responses on gender issues and teacher education, respectively. At early stages of my work, conversations with Reginald Clark, Patricia Edwards, Joyce Epstein, Oliver Moles, and Ruth Nickse were particularly helpful.

Finally, to the many other friends and colleagues whose kind wishes and support cheered me in the writing, and to my family—Michael, who supplied ideas and references, Jonathan, who expressed steady interest, and Gerry, who said the right thing at the right time—heartfelt thanks.

Introduction

I CAME TO WRITE this book because I wanted to share an experience that has been the most meaningful of my professional career. My work in family literacy has meant participating in the process of change, experiencing with others new insights and actions, and coming to a deeper appreciation of the possibilities and problems of this complex field. It was also an adventure, a push into uncharted waters at least in the beginning. The seas were not smooth, but the winds were brisk and exhilarating.

Colleagues, teachers, and family members of schoolchildren were companions on the journey to establish a family literacy program in Newark, New Jersey, schools. I am grateful to have had the opportunity to share their hopes and to have witnessed their achievements, often against great odds. There were mothers who entered public libraries for the first time, who discovered the vital role they could play in their child's education, and who reported improvements in their own literacy development. There was the shy woman who said she didn't get out much, but found friends at the family workshops; and the women who always walked back to their building in the projects together—the way was dangerous. One parent was eager to help lead a family workshop, but came to the session in tears; a relative had broken into her apartment and stolen all the Christmas money. There was also the teacher who planned a family session at her school and when only three mothers showed up checked her disappointment and worked intensively with them for the allotted time. Those mothers couldn't get over it—a teacher taking so much time for them. Later they became the nucleus of a larger group.

This book focuses on the adult participants in family literacy. The reasons for that are twofold; first, my own formative orientation comes from the adult literacy movement and, second, the perspectives of the adult participants, teachers no less than parents, are vital to understanding the significance of family literacy programs and how they might be improved.

1

Given the need for teacher preparation for work in family literacy, it is my hope that this book will provide insight into its complexity and an appreciation of the human face of social issues.

I present the Newark project in the context of family literacy more generally by discussing the issues facing the field and giving examples from research and the experience of projects elsewhere. Issues of gender, social class, and the political environment in which family literacy programs operate are highlighted. The research studies and family literacy projects described are illustrative of the many valuable and interesting efforts in this burgeoning field. Readers are referred to the references for a more comprehensive view.

In this book, I use the term *family member* to represent the significant adult in children's lives out of the recognition that adults other than biological parents may be the primary caregiver. Grandparents, stepparents, foster parents, uncles, aunts, siblings, and others participate in family literacy programs. When stylistic considerations dictate that the word *parent* be used it is meant in an inclusive sense. Since issues of gender are raised in this book, I am careful to indicate whether significant adults are female or male.

Although the focus of this book is on families in poverty whose literacy levels are not high, I believe that affluent or well-educated parents can also benefit from family literacy programs; busy and complex lifestyles often leave little time for fostering their children's literacy development. Over the years, teachers, colleagues, friends, and students have requested booklists or recommendations about how to read to children either for themselves or for others they know. The need is there.

My most active involvement with the Newark project occurred in the years 1987–1995. All descriptions of the school district refer to that time period and not to changes that have occurred since.

ORGANIZATION OF BOOK

This book falls into three main sections. In the first chapter I set out definitional issues, the multiple meanings of the core terms, *literacy* and *family*, and the variables that affect literacy transmission in families. In the second chapter I trace the development of family literacy programs and describe several programs that illustrate factors to be explored in greater depth elsewhere. In Chapter 3, I discuss the new role of the school as a venue for family literacy programs.

I present in Chapters 4–9 the Partnership for Family Reading, a collaborative project of Montclair State University and the Newark, New Jersey,

School District. In Chapter 4 I describe the Newark setting, implementation issues, and the constructivist Family Reading model that guided Partnership activities. Based on interview material, surveys, and participant observation, Chapters 5–8 are analytic narratives of mothers who participated in the project. Drawing on similar empirical data, in Chapter 9 I consider teachers as family literacy learners, including effects of their participation and teacher ownership of the project.

In Chapter 10, in the book's last section, I interweave material from the Partnership into considerations of gender, class, and race as they affect family literacy programs. I discuss in Chapter 11 implications for practice from the Partnership experience, issues in program ownership arising from concepts of family-school collaboration, literacy integration in large-scale programs, and staff development for family literacy. In the final chapter I revisit the social context within which family literacy and all educational programs operate, with specific reference to the new welfare regulations enacted in 1996. The new mandates are reshaping family literacy efforts; I advocate resistance to the narrow goals and unproductive outcomes that may result.

THE RESEARCHER AND THE RESEARCHED: A NOTE ON PROCESS

The mothers interviewed for this book were African American women. As a White, professional, middle-class Jewish woman, I was interviewing across racial, religious, and, in all but one instance, class lines. Omissions, additions, and special presentation may occur in any interview study; I have no doubt that the likelihood of their occurrence was heightened in the current situation. I have wondered also what limitations or perspectives of which I was unaware may have influenced my analysis of the data.

As Roman and Apple (1990) point out, in naturalistic inquiry the relationship between the researcher and the researched affects the account of the particular reality offered by the parties to the research. Feminist as well as naturalist approaches involve a commitment to explain the conditions under which the research process occurred, and to explore the perspectives of the researcher (Harding, 1991; Reinharz, 1992). Accordingly, I offer here a further description of the context in which I as researcher was present.

Following accepted social science practice, my stance as an interviewer was that of an inquirer into the lives of others without knowledge of their particular circumstances or of the influence of the family literacy project on their practices and attitudes. Similarly, the mothers did not know that I was the project developer, although some had seen me in the school and knew that I was from the university. Because of extensive prior contact with other Family Reading participants over the years, I came to the sessions with great respect for women such as those I interviewed—earnest people often working against great odds to make life better for themselves and their children. As a woman who had brought up children under much more privileged circumstances, I admired their taken-for-granted steadfastness and wondered about my own had the burden of race and poverty been added to the usual vicissitudes of child rearing in my case.

I presented myself as open to whatever the mothers wanted to say and made no attempt to channel responses or to curtail long or rambling discourse. Motherhood was a connection between us. I responded to requests to tell about my own personal history ("Do you have children?" "How old are they?") and occasionally offered a personal anecdote to establish connection and stimulate talk. When asked, I gave suggestions about literacy development. Although I attempted to create a pleasant, informal atmosphere in all the interviews, I had the distinct impression that my interview with one of the women, a lawyer, was more relaxed, for both of us. Conversation flowed more smoothly; allusions and references were shared. Her descriptions of her work and educational history were reminiscent of my own, and her portrayal of the nested worlds of literacy in family and community was familiar to me. Another felt difference in the interview was this mother's reflectiveness about her home literacy environment, in contrast to the others, who commented or generalized less frequently about the behaviors they described.

It is important to lay out my own multiple roles: in addition to being the program developer, I was functioning as interviewer and researcher. This situation presented the obvious pitfalls of bias and self-congratulation. However, I believe that three considerations mitigated the danger. First, over the 7 years in which the program had been operating, surveys and informal interviews had confirmed the value of the program as well as some of its limitations. Although in the interviews I asked several questions about the program's effects, program evaluation was not the focus of the interviews. Second, the program had not been static; it bore the influence of others besides myself. The original model had been modified and enlarged by the efforts of teachers with whom I had worked and whom I regarded as ongoing developers. The parents, also, had helped shape the program through surveys and conversations regarding their satisfactions and suggestions for improvement. In addition, my on-site involvement in the school where the interviews were conducted had evolved from my serving as cofacilitator of Partnership for Family Reading workshops the first 2 years, to delivering brief remarks at occasional workshops, to my guest status now—a progressively more distant relationship reflecting the school's successful institutionalization of the program.

I think it pertinent to add that the mothers' descriptions of their home literacy practices evoked memories of my own of more than 2 decades ago. After each interview I found myself noting similarities and differences and reviewing the past from my present vantage point as a literacy researcher, a process that brought some humbling moments. I remembered reading *Curious George* and other enjoyable books, and helping with homework and writing, as did the mothers, but also recalled forgoing other important opportunities for involvement in my children's schooling. Were I and other literacy researchers expecting more from parents today than we had expected from ourselves? I wondered, too, how realistic the expectations for parent involvement in children's education were, and how to fine-tune the relationship between home and school, and when enough was enough. The interviews with mothers in the Partnership for Family Reading became an opportunity for learning on many levels.

CHAPTER 1

The Multiple Meanings of Family Literacy

"TELL ME A STORY, MAMA," begs the child in Angela Johnson's picture book of a mother telling family stories to her 5-year-old daughter. The mother begins and the child joins in, knowing the stories so well that she can almost tell them herself, much as the author, having heard stories over and over from the elders in her own family, had learned to recount them by heart.

These are familiar features of idealized family relationships—a mother and child, well-loved stories, bedtime, an eager audience, an attractive picture book that invites reading aloud. They constitute one meaning of family literacy—an adult, usually a mother, engaged in reading to a child.

A second common practice, also referred to as family literacy, involves programs that familiarize adult caretakers with ways in which to help their children with reading and writing. Drawing on the maxim that parents are a child's first teacher, those programs encourage or educate family members in ways in which to promote the child's academic success.

There is yet another family literacy scenario. Picture an adult, together with other adults, looking at children's books. The adults make predictions about the story and relate events to their own experience. They practice reading aloud together and might mispronounce a word or two. Then they apply reading strategies to materials designed for adults. Later, they incorporate what they have learned when reading with their children. "I learn as much as my child," one says.

These scenes help define perceptions of family literacy, a term that came into public use less than 15 years ago. In the first two scenarios, the adult is viewed as instructor or promoter of the child's development. In the third, both the adult and child are learners. The perspectives are not mutually exclusive; programs under the family literacy rubric may incorporate elements of each. All are informed by the widely endorsed finding that reading aloud to children is the single most important factor in developing

6

their reading proficiency (Anderson, Hiebert, Scott, & Wilkinson, 1985), and by the importance of parents in promoting academic achievement more generally. However, attentiveness to adult literacy improvement is a relatively new component of these programs.

The term *family literacy* is an engaging one, but what does it mean? That question is often asked of researchers and practitioners because definitions are not clear in a field that draws from many disciplines but developed without an explicit theoretical base. At present, there are several overlapping definitions in use. Two relate to interventions, characterized as (a) parent involvement programs whose major purpose is to help parents help their children and also support school learning and (b) intergenerational programs that focus on both child and adult literacy learning, that is, programs that are designed to foster literacy for parents or other adult caretakers as well as children's literacy. The first builds on the well-substantiated concept that significant adults exert influence on children's literacy development; the second definition adds the recognition that literacy or failures to become fully literate tend to perpetuate themselves across generations (Sticht, 1992).

A third definition does not involve programs or interventions, but refers to literacy interactions that occur naturally within home and family. Such interactions have been the subject of much recent research. Although there have been many psychological and sociological studies of family processes, as well as many studies of school-based literacy, researchers have increasingly turned their attention to relationships among family members with respect to literacy and have investigated literacy processes in a diversity of social environments and groups (Delgado-Gaitan, 1990, 1992; Goldenberg, Reese, & Gallimore, 1992; Scott-Jones, 1993; Taylor, 1983; Taylor & Dorsey-Gaines, 1988; Weinstein-Shr, 1990). These scholarly investigations are intended to cast light on family literacy interaction and to help guide programs and practice (Morrow & Paratore, 1993). The focus for all three definitions is on literacy interactions, the behaviors and circumstances that promote sharing or transmission of literacy practices and knowledge among family members.

Family literacy programs are planned and systematic interventions. Those interventions that are intergenerational are planned with the goals of increasing the literacy of both adult and child family members and of helping the adults promote the literacy abilities of the children. Those family literacy programs offer "simultaneous and connected education" for adults and children and in that respect they are unique (Shanahan, Mulhern, & Rodriguez-Brown, 1995, p. 586). In such programs, it is the family that is the unit of interest and the family's function as a learning unit that is the target of the intervention.

Many planned activities sponsored by schools or service organizations help parents foster their children's literacy. Although they might be called family literacy programs, many do not provide simultaneous learning opportunities or attend to adult literacy development in a direct way. Adults may of course pick up incidental literacy learning under such circumstances. However, the family literacy movement originated in an effort to serve all members of the family and the term as used in this book will refer primarily to programs that have an intergenerational goal.

In summary, family literacy is a complex concept that refers to at least three types of activities: intergenerational family literacy programs as described above; parent involvement activities that may or may not be structured programs; and naturally occurring literacy process within families as studied by researchers (Morrow, 1995). Differing goals and pragmatics attach to each. Overall, family literacy draws on the basic social science disciplines of psychology and sociology as reflected in early childhood and emergent literacy development, adult literacy development, learning theory, intergenerational relationships within families, and educational practice.

Intergenerational family literacy programs represent a new and challenging direction for educators. Schools and teachers traditionally focus on children as the beneficiaries of adult effort, rather than on service to the adults themselves, whereas intergenerational programs attempt to serve all members of the family and to meet the needs of adult family members as adult individuals, not just in their role as caregivers for children. In addition, intergenerational programs may challenge the primacy of school learning. Describing underlying premises characteristic of family literacy programs, Gadsden (1994) distinguishes programs that "interpret literacy as the performance of school-like academic activities within family contexts" from those that regard families as sources of information and literacy learning and view literacy practices already used in the home as the basis for instruction (p. 74). One premise asserts the primacy of mainstream academic learning; the other recognizes and values the diversity of literacy practices of different cultural communities. Although these premises are not mutually exclusive and boundaries may blur as programs mature, school-based programs are likely to be oriented toward the former premise at least initially. After all, that is what educators know best. In addition, the literacy activities of the home and the cultural context of home practices are often not readily accessible to school personnel and, in any case, the idea that parents can contribute in a substantial way may seem to challenge professional expertise. Happily, however, many schools and school districts throughout the nation are rising to the challenge in recognition of the need for family literacy programs and because of appreciation of the family's role in promoting literacy.

In this book I will discuss the issues inherent in implementing family literacy programs in schools, from those of the most mundane issues of logistics, to staff development, program content, and the cultural contexts within which programs operate. The multiple factors affecting such programs and the multiple meanings of the program to the participants will be illustrated by descriptions of research and experience in an urban school district, with supplementary descriptions of other programs and research studies. The impact of gender, ethnicity, and social class will be highlighted throughout with reference to the goals and philosophy of family literacy programs, curriculum design, relationships between instructors and participants and between program providers, participants, and the researcher. Reflexivity with regard to the author's voice is intended to accord with feminist methodology that acknowledges the subjectivity of all parties to the research (Reinharz, 1992).

MULTIPLE MEANINGS—LITERACY

That family literacy has different meanings to different people is hardly surprising, since literacy and family are not only elaborated and changing concepts, but ones that involve core emotions. Literacy, the ability to interpret and create written text, is a necessary tool for action in the world. The family is a fundamental social unit and a venue for child socialization. Privileged meanings and beliefs are bound to attach to both.

Literacy involves the communication processes of reading, writing, speaking, and listening, but definitions regard the first element, reading, as primary. Although to some the term connotes only a basic level of skill, the concept is more broadly applied by literacy educators, who regard literacy as a continuum of knowledge and skills ranging from the absence of skills, or illiteracy at the low end of the continuum, to highly sophisticated, critical reading and writing at the high end. In addition, definitions today reflect the purposes of literacy and the need to possess knowledge and skills that are essential for effective functioning within a particular society (Harris & Hodges, 1995). Thus, the mere ability to sign one's name, which marked a person as literate in the American colonies, or attainment of a fourth-grade reading level, which was the hallmark 100 years ago, would hardly suffice as socially relevant in today's technological society, which places a premium upon cognitive rather than manual skills. As society has changed across time, the concept of literacy, that tool for action in the world, has evolved in significant ways. Reflecting current demands, the reading assessment of the National Assessment of Educational Progress puts primacy on analytical skills. Similarly, the National Literacy Act of

1991 defines literacy as "an individual's ability to read, write and speak in English, and to compute and solve problems at levels of proficiency necessary to function on the job and in society" but, in recognition of individual self-direction, adds that the literate person will also demonstrate those abilities necessary "to achieve one's goals, and develop one's knowledge and potential" (Pub. L. No. 102–173, §3). More poetically, Scribner (1988) uses three metaphors to illuminate the profound importance of literacy in human life. She sets forth a multifaceted concept of literacy: as adaptation to societal demands, as power to achieve and to affect society, and as a state of grace, or the enhancement of the self that comes with immersion in the culture of books and learning.

As these broadened definitions suggest, literacy abilities are regarded as developmental, multidimensional in purpose, and sensitive to context; that is, the processes of literacy development are mediated by the individual's interpersonal and social environment as well as by intrapersonal factors or goals. In this view, the ability to interpret and create written text is a process of meaning construction that is shaped by and occurs within a sociocultural context. Located within a social setting, literacy is regarded as a social practice, rather than as merely a set of decontextualized or abstract skills such as decoding symbols to sounds or finding the main idea of a passage. Thus it is possible to think of multiple literacies rather than only one, since literacy practices are developed and exercised in many different life situations and venues and vary in their reasons and purposes. The social-contextual view sees culture, class, race, and gender as shapers of literacy purposes and practices together with more proximal family and intrapersonal factors, which may in turn be influenced by those larger forces. Consider the case of a first grader who was surprised to realize that his parents considered their lively book discussions a reading activity; in school, reading meant a heavy dose of one-right-answer worksheets. Many, but not all, families enjoy a routine of bedtime stories; in cultures where oral expressiveness is highly valued, storytelling rather than book reading may be the norm. Some religious groups eschew stories altogether; sacred texts or factual material are what they value. Traditionally, in the United States, mothers or female teachers have been considered the transmitters of beginning literacy whereas the higher levels of education have been seen as the domain of men. Workplace activities such as reading directions on cleaning supplies, analyzing graphs in a computerized factory, creating a television advertisement, and researching the law are additional examples of literacy practices shaped by distinctive social contexts.

Although the complexity of these concepts may be difficult to convey to a public accustomed to thinking in terms of test scores and basic skills, the social-contextual view is particularly relevant to work in family literacy. The overlapping settings in which literacy is practiced, the linkages to be established between formal and informal institutions, and the influence of parents, teachers, and peers as agents of socialization are consonant with a view of literacy as a set of social practices. The fact that many family literacy programs serve poor or nonmainstream populations whose cultural norms may be unfamiliar to program providers gives particular appropriateness to the concept of literacy as meaning construction within a social context. In addition, the emancipatory uses of literacy in helping individuals understand and change their social conditions (Freire & Macedo, 1987) is also an important part of many family literacy programs.

Family literacy is not a new phenomenon. It is rooted in the long history of the family as a venue for the transmission of knowledge, skills, and values from older to younger generations including, but by no means limited to, those relating to literacy. In 18th-century colonial Boston, Cotton Mather, the Puritan divine, pursued a major purpose for reading that many adults endorse today, the religious instruction of one's children. Reverend Mather read the Bible aloud to his family, told Bible stories at the dinner table, and explicated the significance of Bible text while drawing personally relevant lessons. Among his careful plans for his sons and daughters was the direction to transpose ideas from Scripture and write them down as prayers, an activity requiring the high levels of cognitive processing and critical thinking advocated today (Monaghan, 1991). Notable too is the masculine involvement with higher levels of cognition. At about the same time, an English matron named Jane Johnson had created literacy artifacts to use in teaching her own and neighbors' children. As described and analyzed by Heath (1995), the extensive materials, known as the Nursery Collection, consisted of sets of more than 400 cards with letters, words, and sentences, illustrations from newspapers, blends, original rhymes, and sets of words classified by sound, grammatical function, or meaning. These handmade materials covered all phonic elements and whole-word learning, as well as incorporating story material, contemporary references, and careful matching of illustrations to text.

In her content analysis of the artifacts, Heath (1995) highlights such distinctive qualities as the use of words familiar to children, which she interprets as an intuitive understanding of scaffolding, or providing a bridge from what is known to what a child can do with expert assistance, a Vygotskian (1978) perspective applied in instruction today. Also unusual were the many depictions of working people—not to appear in children's literature until the next century—and of women, particularly working women, whose work is recognized and named. The many social and household references, elements of fantasy, and international references are seen by Heath (1995) as a "multiplicity of voices," another element found in modern research and advocated by proponents of diversity and multicultural understanding.

Although the most direct parallel to these historical examples is the practice of home schooling today, the activities must also resonate with any parent who has read a cautionary fable, made a paper-plate puppet for a young child, pointed out the writing on cereal boxes, or provided magnetic letters and computer programs. We use the technology at hand, and children need no longer be present to be instructed. A colleague, separated from her mother during her childhood, reported that her mother sent her a book through the mail every month; it was her way of maintaining contact and emphasizing the importance of reading. A husband and wife enrolled in a family literacy program read bedtime stories over the telephone to their child in another city. And how many grandmothers are like my friend who videotapes herself reading stories and sends tape and book to her grandchild in another city?

Although family literacy has long been practiced, what is new is the heightened recognition of its importance, research into the complexities of literacy relationships, and the emergence of family literacy programs in schools, adult literacy centers, libraries, and community organizations.

The impetus for the emergence of family literacy programs in the mid-1980s arose from an urgent concern, the need to transform the intergenerational cycle of low achievement operating in the families of many low-literate adults in the nation's poverty areas and the recognition that improving the literacy status of the adult family members must be part of that effort.

This recognition was heralded by business and governmental interests and firmly tied to national economic needs for a better trained workforce in a technological society. Other benefits of literacy, such as personal improvement, empowerment as a citizen, or fulfilling one's role as a family member received less notice. That is, although the achievement of literacy might be an individual good, the impetus for change was directed by concern for national, rather than personal, welfare. With that came an implicit assumption of deficit on the part of low-literate families who did not conform to middle-class or school-like standards of literacy behavior; the literacy activities that did go on in such families and the parents' goals and aspirations for their children tended at first to be overlooked in the thrust for literacy improvement. Today, however, a solid body of research has illuminated the practices of literacy in the homes of low literate, poor, or nonmainstream families. For example, the ethnographic research of Delgado-Gaitan (1990, 1992), Moll (1992), Purcell-Gates (1995), and Taylor and Dorsey-Gaines (1988) investigated literacy lives from the inside, rather than measuring them against an external standard. For these researchers, literacy is valued in the multiple ways in which it occurs. They describe the contexts of family literacy practice, detailing the social networks, norms, and political and economic factors that work to constrain or to foster literacy learning. Sometimes the family practices support or inform school or conventional literacy; other times they seem unrelated. Common to all these studies—and to the experience of adult and family literacy practitioners—is the strength of parents' motivation to foster their children's welfare.

MULTIPLE MEANINGS—FAMILY

Just as concepts of literacy have broadened, understandings about the family have changed. Conventional notions of the permanence and universality of the nuclear family have been challenged by historical analysis and contemporary circumstance. It is now recognized that family structure has always varied by class and culture, and that the model of breadwinner father, stay-at-home mother, both living with their biological children, has represented only one segment of the world's population in the past and remains a restricted model now. In the United States, single-parent families, gay and lesbian families, grandparent families, and "blended" families of stepparents and stepchildren counter that traditional model, as does the range of family structures in other parts of the world. In at least one U.S. state, the judicial definition of family does not include marriage of adult partners; rather, the exclusivity, longevity, and financial and emotional commitment of a relationship, and the members' self-representation to society, are seen as definitive criteria (Stacey, 1994).

The changes in family demographics brought about by social and economic forces will be sketched here only briefly. According to 1997 figures from the Federal Interagency Forum on Child and Family Statistics, the percentage of two-parent families in which both parents worked at year-round full-time jobs increased from 13% to 32% over the past 25 years. Workforce participation by mothers of young children has increased dramatically; more than three fifths of married women with children are in the labor force. In 1950, 6% of the child population lived in mother-only families; that figure quadrupled to 24% in 1990. Demographers report "a drastic decline in the average number of years that men live in households with young children" (Stacey, 1994, p. 657), a circumstance that prompts one to ask where the fathers of those children are and how they fulfill their responsibilities?

Mothers who are young or unmarried are more likely to be poor. The ratio of teen births among Hispanics and African Americans is three times that of Whites. Although, for example, the birth rate for all unmarried African American women has declined in recent years, it substantially exceeds that of other groups, with consequences for health and prenatal care detrimental to the well-being of mother and child (National Center for Health Statistics/NY Times, 1998). Almost one quarter (24.7%) of young children in the United States live in conditions of poverty today (National Center for Children in Poverty, 1998). Shocking, too, is the adolescent mortality rate among Black males, which doubled in a recent 6-year period due to increased use of firearms and now stands at more than twice the mortality ratio of White adolescent males.

The intersection of race, ethnicity, poverty, and education has significant correlation with promotion of literacy. A government report on the prevalence of reading to children in the home states that overall "57 percent of children ages 3–5 were read to daily by a family member" (Federal Interagency Forum on Child and Family Statistics, 1997). However, children were more likely to be read to if their mothers had a higher level of education or if they were living with two parents. With regard to ethnicity and socioeconomic status, the report found that White children were more likely to be read to every day than either Black or Hispanic children and that children in families with incomes below the poverty line were less likely to be read to every day than children in families with higher incomes. "Less than half of the children in poverty were read to every day in 1996, compared to 61% of children above the poverty line" (ibid.).

In addition, the report shows that in less than a decade there has been a doubling of the number of children who have difficulty with English because another language is spoken at home. Like the interrelated factors of minority status and poverty, the diversity of linguistic and immigrant populations have implications for the role of the family, child socialization, education, and public policy. More specifically, under the circumstances, the pressures and practices of family literacy programs may be expected to show considerable variation.

INTERGENERATIONAL INFLUENCES AND CYCLES OF LITERACY

There is extensive documentation of intergenerational influences on literacy and learning. Those influences fall into two broad categories: structural variables, particularly social class; and process variables, or attitudes and actions that appear to foster literacy.

Highlighting the importance of social class, the influential study *Equality of Educational Opportunity* (Coleman et al., 1966) demonstrated that children from low-income families entered school with fewer educational skills than children from higher income families and that the gap widened with each year of school. Of particular significance for the family literacy movement was the growing evidence that cycles of low literacy tend to repeat themselves across generations. For example, the 1985 National Assessment of Educational Progress reported a positive correlation between level of parental education, particularly the mother's, and the literacy achievement of children. A further analysis of the National Assessment of Educational Progress showed that 8th- and 12th-grade students who had access to a variety of reading materials at home and who reported that their family members read a lot had higher average proficiencies in reading than students for whom the opposite was true (Foertsch, 1992, p. 28). Having access to books in the home and living in a home where adults or siblings read frequently are important factors in the development of reading achievement. Where parental education is high, adults are more likely to model a variety of literacy practices, know how to deploy strategies that promote school learning, and be able to provide resources. Arguably, contingent on their reading facility, such parents may also possess a greater store of general knowledge and with it the elaborated mental schema, which if accessible and internalized, enhances their children's likelihood of greater reading development (Vygotsky, 1978).

Education, together with occupation and income, form the construct known as social class or socioeconomic status. Since ethnic minorities are disproportionately poor, it is important not to confound the effects of ethnicity and social class. Regardless of ethnicity, the positive correlation of maternal education level with children's reading proficiency holds true (Kirsch & Jungeblut, 1986). However, children from poor, nonmainstream backgrounds are less likely to have the advantages of living with highly educated adults and, on average, perform less well on measures of reading comprehension than their more privileged peers. Accordingly, the attained achievement of children varies by ethnic group, with Whites scoring higher than African-American, Hispanic, or Native American children. These discrepancies reflect the inequalities in our society and the continuing need for large-scale remedies of the conditions of disadvantage.

FAMILY PROCESSES

Structural variables do not tell the whole story, however. Another important intergenerational influence on literacy and learning relates to family processes, and many people can recount examples of the critical difference made by a parent who valued or supported their education. One story of many involves a reading instructor with an advanced degree; he tells of his mother who had only a rudimentary education and did not speak English but insisted he do his homework before going out to play; she sat with him in the kitchen providing moral authority and affection as he completed work she could not understand.

A brief sketch of literacy influence in families begins on the most basic level with children learning speech as their caretakers talk and interact spontaneously with them; later, they watch their parents' and siblings' literacy behaviors and may use them as a model for their own. In a more planned way, adults in the family shape children's opportunities for literacy engagement; for example, adults may read to children because both they and the child find it an enjoyable and appropriate activity; other informal literacy activities such as library visits, or writing notes or shopping lists, may be embedded in the family experience. On the most formal level, adults in the family may set out deliberately to act as teachers of their children. Expectations and attitudes toward literacy, family routines, and resources of information and experience—the social capital that the family can provide—affect the growing child's literacy development, as does the interpersonal environment within the family.

Hannon (1995) has categorized four major types of family process that promote children's literacy development: opportunities, recognition, interaction, and modeling. *Opportunities* for learning include exposure to literacy resources and also the active intervention of the parent in interpreting and sharing the experience. *Recognition* of children's efforts involves the parental role as encourager and rule-maker. *Interaction* highlights the importance of the interpersonal relationship; parents need to interact with children, supporting, explaining, involving them in real literacy tasks, and "challenging them to move on from what they know about literacy to do more" (p. 51). Specific activities under these first three categories will vary according to the child's developmental stage. Finally, *modeling* refers to parental behaviors as literacy users and learners themselves.

Operationally, how does the intergenerational transfer of literacy from adult to child come about? Analyzing the research on this issue, Snow and Tabors (1996) identify four mechanisms of literacy transfer. The first is *simple transfer* of print skills through picture book reading to young children, functional writing such as in shopping lists, and directing attention to print resources in the home and outside environments. The second means of transfer from one generation to another is termed *participation in literacy practice*. This view is grounded in a definition of literacy as social practice embedded in a wide range of social contexts. According to this view, the parents facilitate access to literacy practices that children can participate in as important parts of their lives; regular library visits, recourse to text for directions for doing something, and writing as a means of obtaining or exchanging information are ready examples. Parents also model literacy as a practice that is useful to adults. Drawing on their own research, Snow and Tabors also discuss intergenerational transfer via *linguistic and cognitive mechanisms*. This research highlights the influence of extended, decontextualized discourse during family activities as a predictor of children's later reading achievement. Noncontextualized talk, that is, reference to events or situations that are not concretely present, and elaborated discussions in which connections to background knowledge, explanations, or feelings are made fosters cognitive abilities that are important for higher level reading comprehension. The research by Snow et al. (1991) indicates that children who have opportunities to hear or provide extended text at home "build skills in producing extended discourse of precisely the type that is needed for high levels of literacy" (p. 77) and that such opportunities are better predictors of reading achievement than parental practice of simply reading aloud.

The fourth category of literacy transfer is *enjoyment and engagement*, which can reasonably be present in all intergenerational transactions, or so one hopes. Snow and Tabors (1996) discuss it as a mechanism for intergenerational transfer that might help to explain individual differences among children from similarly literate families. Presumably, positive affect toward books, including individual attention from parents who find reading a source of enjoyment and enjoy reading to their children, helps children persist in the acquisition of beginning reading skills; later their expectation of enjoyment "leads to more time spent reading, i.e. more practice, and thus greater fluency—a major predictor of long-term reading outcomes" (p. 76). Engagement and enjoyment may be particularly important for children from disadvantaged groups, who have less reason to believe that literacy will serve them as a route to school or occupational success.

Contrary to common assumption, literacy transmission is not always unidirectional, from adult to child. In immigrant populations where English-language proficiency is an issue, transmission often runs in a reverse direction as the children interpret the English-speaking world for the adults. Influence can be reciprocal and recursive as children respond, react, and initiate, and thereby influence adult behavior in turn. For example, parents engaging in interactive book reading with their children have remarked on their child's interest and then taken further steps to develop it (Handel, 1992). A related assumption of the unidirectional transmission model is that the sole focus of interest in literacy interaction is the child.

FAMILIES, SCHOOLS, COMMUNITIES

Voluminous evidence that family involvement in children's education fosters school achievement has been summarized by Henderson and Berla

(1994). With specific reference to reading, a study by Epstein (1991) reports that when teachers involved parents in reading activities with their children, the children showed greater reading gains than those whose parents were not involved. A British project demonstrated the power of parent involvement of a minimal sort; when children in multiethnic schools read to their parents, many of whom did not understand English, their progress in reading was significantly greater than groups given extra school-reading instruction. Other effects of this literacy sharing were greater interest in schoolwork on the part of the children, and continued relationships between parents and teachers (Tizard, Schofield, & Hewison, 1982).

A 1996 report by the U.S. Department of Education, *Reading Literacy in the United States*, further confirms the importance of parental involvement; where parental involvement was judged to be high, reading scores of fourth graders were above the national average; where parental involvement was low, reading scores fell below the national average. The phenomenon did not vary with the level of parental education, suggesting that under favorable conditions, such as effective outreach by the school, less-well-educated parents can have a positive influence on their children's school achievement. In general, however, students whose parents had less than a high school education had below-average reading comprehension scores. This is the intergenerational cycle, or reproduction of low school achievement, that family literacy programs seek to interrupt.

Large-scale surveys present averages; they do not predict individual performance. Simplistic explanations of such survey findings may criticize "different" home environments, or assume cognitive "deficiencies" on the part of schoolchildren, and predict low-paying jobs and the perpetuation of low literacy in their families in the future. This is not only a deterministic view but one that tends to blame poor families for their socioeconomic position. As is usual in human affairs, matters are considerably more complicated. The cycle of poverty does not operate in the same way for all families, nor for that matter does the cycle of advantage for more privileged families (Lareau, 1989), and there are multiple points where the cycle may be interrupted.

As discussed by Scott-Jones (1992), it is incorrect to assume that all low-income minority families will affect their children in the same manner; variability exists in self-definition, practices, and patterns of communication, thus creating home environments that vary widely in support of intellectual development. Individual children may or may not show the pattern of strengths and deficiencies associated with group membership. A case in point is Clark's (1983) ethnographic study, *Family Life and School Achievement: Why Poor Black Children Succeed or Fail*, showing the variability in family routines and support in the homes of high school students and its effect on school achievement.

In addition to cognitive skills, family variables affect children's motivation, social skills, and underlying mental and physical health, all of which interact with schooling. Moreover, the characteristics of the school and curriculum itself, the relationship between parents and school, and the peer environment may also mediate school achievement (Scott-Jones, 1993). Scott-Jones points out that children's school experiences can serve as either risk or protective factors, exacerbating dysfunctional aspects of their lives or providing experiences that build hope and achievement. She cogently argues that poverty also affects schools directly, since schools in poverty neighborhoods have a lower tax base for resources. Poor schools for poor children lower the quality of children's school experiences and lessen their life chances.

Additional community factors that may serve as protections or risks in the cycle of poverty include the opportunity for employment and economic mobility offered or perceived to be offered by society, which may influence motivation to achieve in school. In Ogbu's (1988) study, young people saw no reason to exert effort to do well; their poverty neighborhoods had high rates of unemployment and offered few opportunities regardless of level of education. Although the opportunity structure of society mediates level of education and employment, it is not a fixed entity. To the extent that they exist in poverty neighborhoods, social organizations such as Boys and Girls Clubs, public libraries, and religious institutions may function as sources of information and wider perspectives. Immigrants have often praised public libraries for opening up new worlds and raising aspirations; they are centers of information and inspiration today. Mario Puzo, author of *The Godfather*, who grew up in a low-literate home, credits a settlement house with broadening his horizons and helping him move out of poverty. These social institutions may counter, supplement, or reinforce home and school experiences, and serve as another point of intervention into the cycle of poverty.

It is important to recognize that the earlier immigrants, however poor, perceived this country as a land of opportunity and, to an extent, were correct in their perceptions. In contrast, the experience of people of color has been restricted by racism. Today, racism, entrenched conditions of poverty, and the growing polarization between the poor and working poor and the more affluent segments of society demand advocacy from the education community to ameliorate conditions that greatly affect children's learning and adult capabilities. Family literacy programs have been seen as one way to do that. Whether or not they can fulfill that large promise remains an open question.

CHAPTER 2

Development of Family Literacy Programs

PLANNED INTERVENTIONS TO PROMOTE family literacy emerged in the 1980s, stimulated by national concern about the literacy skills of people in poverty, and supported by advocacy efforts directed to public agencies and Congress. These efforts emphasized the intergenerational nature of literacy learning and the benefits that could result from directing resources to adult as well as child education (Ford Foundation, 1988; Sticht, 1992). Many programs, such as the pioneering Collaborations for Literacy in Boston in 1984 (Nickse & Englander, 1985), originated within the adult literacy practitioner community, long devoted to raising the literacy and economic status of adults and aware that many adult learners were strongly motivated by the desire to help their children with reading and schoolwork. New in adult literacy programs was the focus on children and the attentiveness to the adult learner in his—or more usually her—role as parent. Although the early family literacy programs were guided by principles of adult and child learning, by and large they were pragmatic responses to felt needs and opportunities, rather than derived from prior extensive research. The vision of all, however, was of child and parent as a "learning team" (Nickse, 1990, p. 5) directed toward the goal of breaking the intergenerational cycle of low literacy. Simultaneously during this period, early childhood interventions were beginning to focus on the family, as well as the child, although literacy was not usually a prime concern.

The growth of family literacy programs was fueled by federal legislation such as the Adult Education Act, Head Start, library legislation, the Family Support Act, Title I, and notably the Even Start Family Literacy Act, whose sole aim is the promotion of family literacy. The first state-sponsored effort to break the cycle of undereducation through a joint program of preschool learning and adult skill development was established by Kentucky in 1986. Its Parent and Child Education Program, a marriage of early childhood and adult education, shaped the model for the National

Center for Family Literacy and the federal Even Start program. In 1988, authorization of Even Start (now the Even Start Family Literacy Program) provided federal funding exclusively for intergenerational programs; it is now the most widespread family literacy effort, with more than 900 projects serving families in the 50 states.

Also helping to launch the new movement was the Barbara Bush Foundation for Family Literacy, created in 1989 and headed by the former first lady. Through Barbara Bush's well-publicized reading sessions with children, the issue was put before the general public in a clear and popular way. Another influential organization, the Business Council for Effective Literacy, promoted business sector support of intergenerational programs by emphasizing the importance of a skilled workforce. The major adult literacy organizations, Laubach Literacy and Literacy Volunteers of America, added family literacy to their training programs.

The family literacy programs were directed to low-income, undereducated families in urban and rural settings. From the beginning, they varied in type and scope of services, sponsorship, level of available resources, and whether the intervention focused on adults, children, or both.

Reading books to children was a major component of most of the early programs. For example, in 1986, the pioneering intergenerational program developed by Nickse and her associates (Nickse, Speicher, & Buchek, 1988) established a community center in Boston for literacy services in which adults participated in adult basic education and read storybooks to their children. The Mothers' Reading Program, sponsored by the American Reading Council in New York in 1984, was primarily directed to adults, although children attended special events and borrowed books from the community storefront in a Spanish-speaking neighborhood. Based on the philosophy of Paulo Freire, this program helped women create group stories centered on immediate concerns and issues in their lives. The English Family Literacy Project, which began in 1986 with funds from the U.S. Office of Bilingual Education and Minority Language Affairs, is another large project based on Freire's principles in which adult learners explore critical issues in their lives and use literacy as tool for empowerment (Auerbach, 1989).

Building on the concept of children's literature as a vehicle for adult literacy improvement and as a means to encourage parents to read to their children, in 1986 Handel and Goldsmith established Parent Reader workshops for developmental reading students at a community college in New York (Handel & Goldsmith, 1988). At about the same time, Kentucky educators established the Parent and Child Education program (PACE) to provide both generations with literacy and related experiences together at the same site. In 1987, in a Louisiana school, Edwards established Parents as Partners in Reading, which taught parents who had not grown up in a book environment how to read to their elementary school children.

Also in the late 1980s, Beginning with Books, based in the Carnegie Library in Pittsburgh, established a unified service of adult literacy tutoring, developmental services for children, and family book borrowing. Another library program by the Marin County (California) Library provided at-home adult literacy tutoring and bookmobile services for Mexican farmworker families. MOTHERREAD, Inc. in North Carolina helped incarcerated mothers and, later, fathers communicate with their children through book sharing. Other organizations, such as Take Up Reading Now in Washington, DC, the Family Learning Centers of SER-Jobs for Progress in several states, and the Avance Parent-Child Education program in Texas reinforced or added some literacy components to their ongoing family support programs.

The forerunner programs continue today, many in expanded form. The National Center for Family Literacy now conducts training in its model nationwide. A private organization, the National Center plays an influential role in public policy as well. Its Kenan model has four main components—early childhood education, adult literacy, parenting education, and joint parent and child activities. The smaller scale programs of Handel and Goldsmith and Edwards continue, having expanded to schools, preschools, and community sites throughout the country. The availability of federal Family Literacy Library funds has stimulated library programs nationwide. Title I regulations now make outreach to families a school responsibility in accordance with the National Education Goal of family-school partnerships. Hawai'i has pioneered statewide family literacy efforts; in many states family literacy is included in goals and regulations for adult literacy. (For descriptions of forerunner and current programs see Barbara Bush Foundation for Family Literacy, 1989; McIvor, 1990; Morrow, 1995; and Morrow, Tracey, & Maxwell, 1995; Nickse, 1990.)

Even Start, the most extensive program, has since 1992 been administered by state education agencies; many of its projects are located in the public schools. Even Start goals are to help parents become full partners in the education of their children; to assist children in reaching their full potential; and to provide literacy training for the adults (McKee & Rhett, 1995). Participants are low-income families with children under 8 years of age. The Even Start model calls for the integration of early childhood education, adult basic education, and parenting education. Family participation in all three core components is required. Projects must also include home visits and joint parent-child activities. The collaboration of many school, social, and community agencies is required to provide an intensive, unified program that builds on, rather than duplicates, existing services.

Even Start mandates a structure, but does not specify curriculum activities or the mechanisms of collaboration (McKee & Rhett, 1995). Many variations exist in those areas.

The great majority of programs are directed toward families with young children; parents have a strong influence on language and literacy development, and early experiences set patterns. Yet older students also rely on family support and their parents may have needs of their own. Projects involving older students take different forms and raise different issues. A family literacy program in a Baltimore middle school provided literacy and parenting education to adults and homework help to students (Connors, 1994). Parents' skills improved and their confidence as educators of their children increased, but it proved difficult to engage the middle school children in many of the joint parent-student activities that were planned. An Australian program at the secondary school level offered workshops for adults on study skills, which they would then teach their youngsters at home (Cairney, 1995). The adults learned new ways to help with schoolwork, the students acquired new skills, and both reported improved family relationships. Interestingly, the program evolved from the requests of parents who had participated in an earlier program for elementary school families.

Today, as a result of advocacy, funding, and publicity, family literacy programs are operating in schools, preschools, adult literacy centers, community organizations, libraries, prisons, workplaces, and shelters for the homeless and victims of domestic violence. Family literacy is featured at conferences of major professional organizations, such as the International Reading Association, National Reading Conference, and American Association for Adult and Continuing Education. The National Center for Family Literacy holds an annual conference devoted to the topic. Included under the family literacy rubric are many types of programs serving different populations with varying levels of resources. There are hundreds of programs at the local level, some school based, some community based, that are described as family literacy programs.

Given the multiplicity of programs, a systematic way to characterize this proliferating field was needed. Nickse (1990) developed a typology that categorized programs according to intensity of intervention and type of participant:

1. Direct services to both adults and children, embodied in a curriculum of integrated intensive services (typified by the Even Start Family Literacy model and the work of the National Center for Family Literacy)
2. Indirect services to both adults and children with less intensive par-

ticipation or little instruction (book fairs, author readings and similar literacy enrichment events)

3. Direct services to adults, indirect services to children (literacy workshops for adults as in Collaborations for Literacy, the Parent Readers Program, and Family Reading; children participate less frequently, but benefit from adult expertise)

4. Direct services to children, indirect services to adults (the child is the primary beneficiary as in Head Start or in school programs in which parents may be asked to participate in reading to children or helping with homework, but receive little instruction)

DESCRIPTIONS OF SELECTED PROGRAMS

Three intergenerational programs are described below to give some flavor of family literacy in operation. The first two comprehensive programs provide integrated services that address their participants' social needs within the literacy context. The third, smaller program focuses on staff development as well as workshops for family members. All illustrate themes to be explored later in this book.

HACKENSACK C.A.R.E.S.—AN EVEN START PROGRAM

One comprehensive and long-running program is the Hackensack, New Jersey, Community Activities Reinforcing Even Start (C.A.R.E.S.), now in its 7th year. It is an example of a well-integrated program in which even the bus drivers who provide transportation take an active part. Collaborating with an area college, the YMCA, public library, and other community organizations, this public school–based program serves a poor, largely Spanish-speaking population of about 105 families each year. At least 50% of the families have been in the program more than 2 years.

The program operates in the evenings and on Saturdays; parents and children go to school together. English as a second language as well as parenting activities and reading, writing, and numeracy instruction are provided for the adults. Computer-aided instruction is a program highlight and laptops are available for home use. Preschool activities for the children center around a whole-language approach based on the district's curriculum guide. Social activities for the entire family, such as trips and potluck dinners, are a third program strand. In addition, the staff makes weekly home visits with follow-up material. Each family receives 10 books a year for their home library plus subscriptions to a children's magazine and a bilingual newsletter. A social service liaison assists families with referrals to community agencies.

Some of the adults are literate in their home language, but need intensive English training; a few, virtually illiterate, need to be taught to write their names. Several graduates of the program have obtained their general equivalency diploma and gone on to study at a community college; others are working as program staff, a sure sign of the enthusiasm and competence that the program engenders. Children who have been in the program are reported to be functioning well in school.

As with many family literacy programs, the majority of adult participants are women. Many are isolated women who have found friends in the program. According to the C.A.R.E.S. director (R. Ackerman, personal communication, July 22, 1997) this sociability and mutual support are important factors in recruiting and maintaining participants in the program. Another important factor is program flexibility; activities are responsive to the different cultures within the Spanish-speaking population and to the needs of participants as they arise. For example, when changes in the immigration law stimulated an increase in citizenship applications, the staff helped participants to fill out the necessary papers and accompanied them to the appropriate agencies. Trust is the basic principle that makes the program work, Ackerman (1997) emphasizes; trust starts slowly and builds up over the years, as participants realize that the staff does what is promised and is always there to help.

Even Start is not a quick fix. The life stresses of participants who work at multiple, low-paying jobs and care for large families necessitate realistic goals. Learner progress to high-school-level literacy may take years; program viability is a slow and cumulative process as the staff becomes increasingly knowledgeable through experience. Ackerman (personal communication, July 22, 1997) maintains that Hackensack C.A.R.E.S. is not transportable in the sense of packaged lesson plans. However, the principles of support, program flexibility, and trust can surely guide other programs.

SHIPROCK, NEW MEXICO—THE KENAN MODEL

Both Even Start and programs implementing the Kenan model of the National Center for Family Literacy (which include many Even Start projects) fit the Nickse (1990) typology of intensive and integrated direct services to both adults and children. As described by Potts and Paull (1995), the Kenan model offers comprehensive services of early childhood education, adult literacy, parenting sessions, and parent-child joint activities; volunteering in the child's school is included as well. The National Center has trained family literacy staff in every part of the country, including 22 sites serving Native American populations.

In an elementary school building on the Navaho reservation in Shiprock, New Mexico, two classrooms stand side by side. Separated only by a small hallway, one classroom serves the adult education participants, the other their children, ages 3 to 8. The classrooms' proximity is a tangible illustration of the program's ethos of integrated services to families. The hallway is often used for joint parent-child activities. The program operates 4 days a week for a full day. In addition, a home-based program for families with children under age 3 is provided. Some parents volunteer in elementary school classrooms even when their children are no longer in the program.

While preschool children are involved in the High Scope curriculum, their family members—overwhelmingly mothers—are engaged in parenting and literacy-based activities. An example of a health literacy project that emerged out of felt needs is their training in cardiopulmonary resuscitation (CPR). Participants read CPR materials in the adult education classes, then practice the technique. Sometimes children participate in the practice. The training leads to CPR certification.

The Shiprock program has been in existence for 8 years. As with most family literacy programs of any duration, it has gone through an evolutionary process. According to Dr. Meta Potts, the National Center's former director of training and staff development, negotiating cultural differences took time. As in many situations of cultural diversity, a significant task for instructors, who were mainly Caucasian when the project began, was to learn how to be sensitive to the culture of a group not their own and to understand, for example, that not every group addresses family issues such as discipline in the same way. Now, there are more Navaho instructors on staff. Another issue is the availability of textual material in Navaho. Although Native American languages are becoming more predominant in the Southwest, Navaho has been an oral culture and the language did not exist in written form until recently. Children's books in Navaho have been difficult to find. Some culturally appropriate books in English have been translated by those individuals who can read and write in Navaho. Teachers and parents have also written books together in the Navaho language for use in the program.

The aspect of the program most congenial to Navaho culture is the family focus. The adults see family literacy as a way of keeping the family together and of having a chance to do something for themselves that does not entail letting go of their child. The fact that children participate in the program with them is a big plus (Potts, personal communication, July 24, 1997).

READING STARTS WITH US—THE FAMILY READING MODEL

Reading Starts with Us, a privately funded program for families with children of preschool age through first grade, focuses on direct services to adults and indirect services to children (Nickse's Type 3 model) and is a less extensive intervention than the two programs described. Since 1990, Reading Starts with Us has trained day care, Head Start and early childhood teachers from 41 agencies and schools that serve low-income families in poverty areas of New York City. More than 600 parents have participated in program workshops and more than 1,000 children have benefited from the enriched literacy experiences that their parents have learned to provide.

Reading Starts with Us is a two-tier program. First, teachers receive extensive training in Goldsmith and Handel's (1990) Family Reading model; then they conduct a four-session series of workshops for adult family members. By preparing teachers to provide family literacy workshops and helping them assume the role of parent educator, the program enables parents to foster their children's literacy development and promote academic success. The parent workshops focus on book reading and discussion. With the support of the trained educators, parents learn how to use interactive reading strategies when reading to their children and how to create a literacy-rich environment at home. Quality children's books are available for home reading.

Among the benefits that teachers have gained from the program are greater familiarity with children's literature, presentation skills, and greater understanding of other cultures. Closer contact with parents was a common theme. Asked what she found most valuable, one teacher replied:

> How to deal with parents and getting them interested in their children's reading at home. The sharing and discussions. Learning from each other.

In a recent development, the program has reached out to neighborhood libraries in order to promote access to books in an ongoing way and to provide families with multiple supports for literacy development. Librarians have participated in staff development sessions and will provide book talks at parent workshops. Libraries will also host participating families to introduce them to the children's collection and adult books of interest and to issue library cards. According to Dr. Ellen Goldsmith, Reading Starts with Us director, this initiative also has been enthusiastically received by parents, librarians, and teachers and has deepened connections with the surrounding communities.

This sampling of school-based programs directed toward families with young children illustrates but by no means exhausts the variety of family literacy projects. The three programs do, however, touch on important themes to be explored in greater depth. They include the valuing of language and culture (as in the Shiprock example); social-class status of the participants; gender issues (the great majority of teachers and parents were women); the ways in which programs address needs and values of participants (family closeness in Shiprock, sociability and immigration procedures in C.A.R.E.S.); outcomes for participants; staff development (most fully described in Reading Starts with Us); and program flexibility and growth.

Far from being schematic, restricted curriculum efforts, the family literacy programs are grounded in the human environments of home, community, and personal life. They address circumstances of poverty, culture, race, gender, social-class differences between service providers and family members, and the effects on program design and philosophy, all factors that have implications for the research and policy as well as program levels. In addition, many issues of how and by whom literacy is transmitted in families remain to be explored. Apparent thus far is the importance of understanding the home situations and cultural norms of participating families and the place of literacy within them. Recommendations from ethnographic research studies have yielded insights to inform policy and practice. Implied in such recommendations is the need to obtain the perspectives of program participants, and to recognize them as sources of information and as subjects of their own learning so that the emancipatory possibilities of family literacy may be achieved.

CHAPTER 3

Family Literacy in Schools

"SPEAK UP SO EVERYONE can hear you," said the kindergarten teacher to the little girl. It was the first week of school; the teacher had just asked a question and the child had responded to her quietly, as if in a private conversation at home. Observing the interaction, I saw the bewildered look on the child's face. Response as public performance was not yet in her repertoire.

This incident is a typical example of the discontinuity that children experience when making the transition from the personal voice of home or preschool to the public routines of formal schooling. Not seen by the school, but equally operative, is the impact on the adults at home as the school places new demands on family life, such as adaptation to schedules, homework, monitoring of progress, and assessment by outsiders. As Lightfoot (1978) and others have noted when comparing the different perspectives of school and home, schools are expected to take a universalist, impartial stance toward all students whereas parents' interests are vested in their own individual children. Family literacy activities, too, are colored by personal relations, as in the warmth of a bedtime story for example, and are likely to be more multifaceted. Involving children in the family shopping may involve conversation about what is needed, reading supermarket ads or coupons, writing the shopping list, and reading product labels while shopping. This embeddedness in activity and seamless flowing from one literacy element to another contrasts with the segmentation of literacy learning in many school curricula.

Differences of culture and language complicate the picture further. Teachers may not be familiar with home activities related to literacy development, cultural variation in home activities, or their possible influence on school achievement. Parents who have limited English-language skills or who are used to deferring to teachers as authorities may not respond readily to requests for participation in school activities. When home and school come together in family literacy programs, the issue of negotiating differences and familiarities is especially marked.

Family literacy is a new and challenging direction for schools. Among the challenges are

- the differing structures of school and home—the one bureaucratic, the other informal—and the need to understand and adjust those differences in the interest of true collaboration;
- the need for teachers and schools to direct efforts toward the whole family as a learning unit, not just the child;
- changes in teachers' role to that of family educator;
- questions of appropriate pedagogy, materials, and relationships with regard to adult learning styles, experience, and values;
- expectations and cultural norms of educators as well as those of families that need to be explicated and understood;
- provision of staff development, since teacher and administrator preparation has not typically included instruction in how to conduct effective family programs; and
- ethical considerations related to efforts to change family lifestyles.

In addition, family literacy programs represent a break with past practice. Although school personnel overwhelmingly agree that parent involvement is a compelling need, relationships with parents have been mixed at best as educators have been careful to guard their professional turf. More recently, schools have begun to act on the necessity for vigorous outreach to the families of their students, especially in poverty areas where populations may not be as oriented to school as those in more affluent neighborhoods.

HOME-SCHOOL RELATIONS AND FAMILY LITERACY

Family literacy in schools is one aspect of home-school relations. Whether family literacy is a small stand-alone program in a school, or part of a large restructuring effort involving an entire school or district, it reflects the obstacles and opportunities of home-school relations more generally.

Summarizing the history of parent involvement in education, Moles (1993) points out that the role of parents as educators diminished in the United States as schooling became professionalized in the late 19th and early 20th century. Parent organizations that had been operating earlier, seeking such progressive reforms as better sanitation, school lunches, and services to the poor, were opposed by wealthy taxpayers who feared greater dependence among the poor, and by school officials who feared

encroachment on school prerogatives (p. 23), criticisms that have resonance today.

As Moles (1993) points out, legitimatization of parent involvement
came with the social programs of the 1960s. Head Start trained mothers
in home-teaching methods, solicited parent input in program planning and
used parent paraprofessionals in program operations. The Elementary and
Secondary School Education Act of 1964 funded compensatory education
programs for schools serving low-income children and mandated parent
advisory councils, although specific regulations were weakened in subsequent decades. These reforms did not come about in a social vacuum. Facilitated by an expanding economy, the Great Society measures were responses to the civil rights movement; national investigations of poverty in
the United States; child development research that stressed the influence of
families; and the feminist movement of the 1970s, which criticized schools
as perpetuating gender stereotypes. Also in the 1970s the disabilities rights
movement organized, resulting in the Education for All Handicapped Children Act, which mandated a parental role in designing educational programs. All created an atmosphere receptive to increased parent participation in education.

Although these initiatives recognized the importance of parent involvement in education, their thrust was the amelioration of the effects of poverty and the improvement of children's education, rather than the promotion of intergenerational learning. Adult literacy could be a by-product, but
was not the focus, of teaching parents how to stimulate their young children, or involving them as paraprofessionals in the schools, or encouraging
them to participate in educational policy and decision making. In subsequent years, conflicts over school governance and intractable problems of
poverty led some educators to focus on variables that schools could change,
for example stressing safe and orderly environments within the school
building, clear expectations for student performance, and coherent curricula, rather than on external forces over which they felt they had little control. Overall, according to Moles (1993, p. 28) few schools worked actively
in the 1970s and 1980s to foster parent participation in the instructional
process. Then as now fewer contacts with schools were maintained by families of lower socioeconomic status than by their better-off counterparts.

In recent years, policy directives have placed the school's role in promoting family involvement high on the national education agenda. In acknowledgment of the school's responsibility to reach out to families, the
Goals 2000: Educate America Act of 1994 directs every school to "promote partnerships that will increase parental involvement and participation
in promoting the social, emotional, and academic growth of children."
Other goals propose that by the year 2000 "every child will start school

ready to learn" and "every adult American will be literate and will possess the knowledge and skills necessary to compete in a global economy and exercise the rights and responsibilities of citizenship" (National Education Goals Panel, http://www.negp.gov). Taken together, these goals support the development of family literacy programs in schools.

Other federal initiatives include regulations incorporating family literacy into Head Start; funds for America Reads tutors in family literacy programs; a mandate that schools in low-income areas receiving Title I funds create compacts to involve parents in shared responsibility for student achievement; continued support of the Even Start Family Literacy program; and sponsorship of a Partnership for Family Involvement in Education in conjunction with more than 2,000 education, community, business, parent, and religious organizations with the aim of involving them in activities that support schools and foster children's academic progress. Literacy is a major focus. A summer program, READ*WRITE*NOW, supplies kits and suggestions for tutors of young children. Research summaries, manuals of activities, newsletters, and overviews of federal, state, and community efforts in family literacy are available from the U. S. Department of Education web site (http://www.ed.gov) and in hard copy publication.

It is safe to assume that throughout these swings of the pendulum, played out in varying degrees among the nation's 15,000 school districts, elementary school teachers were exhorting parents to read to their children. Teachers have always known the value of reading to children. What is new now is that schools have recognized that simple exhortation is rarely sufficient. Parents across the socioeconomic spectrum may need increased access to and familiarity with books, enhanced skills in book reading, and recognition of the benefits of many other literacy-related practices. Families also may not be sufficiently aware of the importance of supporting their children's literacy or may overlook it in the press of busy lives. Far from wishing to exclude parent and community resources, educators began to realize that schools could not go it alone.

Undergirding these new understandings are ecological theories of learning that identify the multiple and interdependent contexts within which learning occurs. Home, community, school, peer group, workplace and religious organizations as well as other formal and informal social groups all may be contexts for literacy learning. This greater recognition of contexts for learning outside school has also promoted the importance of family and community involvement in education. Although the school has a vital role to play, it is accepted that multiple factors affect literacy development. Research that viewed these contexts as separate or competing influences on children's learning in the 1960s has been superseded by studies that embrace the concept of shared responsibility (Epstein, 1987, 1995).

The new understandings of literacy learning recognize that parents are children's first teachers and that literacy experiences in the home prior to school entry are an important factor in subsequent learning. School is no longer seen as the point at which children acquire literacy or the only literacy-fostering agent. Rather, literacy is regarded as a developmental process starting at the earliest ages and continuing to develop throughout the lifespan, responsive to many influences both in and out of school. Family and community are important influences on preschool children's emergent literacy, in other words, knowledge about written text before formal decoding skills are acquired; during school years and thereafter, the support of family, community, and peers continue to be influential in literacy growth. Viewed as a lifelong process, literacy continues to develop in multiple ways throughout the adult lifespan.

Some of these insights reflect earlier ones. As long ago as 1908, Huey, the prominent educational psychologist, spoke of the importance of parents to the literacy learning of their children. More recently, Leichter's (1984) important ethnographic studies described how families provided an environment for literacy. What is different now is the acceptance of their message and its urgency.

UNDERSTANDING THE NEW ROLE OF SCHOOLS

Connections with families and communities are seen as part of the broader movement to improve schools and student performance. As Epstein (1991) points out, the main question has changed, moving from "Are families important for student success in school? to *If* families are important for children's development and school success, *how* can schools help all families conduct the activities that will benefit their children?" (p. 213). Placing common responsibility on researchers and educators, Epstein goes on to raise a series of related questions:

> What do we need to know and do to help all children succeed in school and to enable their families to help them do so? How can schools communicate with families and community groups to enable more families to guide their children on positive paths, from birth through high school? How can communications be family friendly, feasible for schools, and acceptable to students? What are the effects of alternative designs and implementation processes of practices of partnership? (p. 213)

Working out answers to these questions is bound to be complex. Answers will vary with local conditions, including resources, demographics, type of school, and the ages of students served, as well as with changing times that require new thinking. There is no one right solution. The operative concept, however, is one of partnership between school and home, a "new vision" for schools that have traditionally avoided mutuality in their relations with parents (Swap, 1993, p. 58). Family literacy programs, situated as they are in many different venues, including many different types of schools serving different populations and providing different human and material resources, face these same questions. In addition, they face the complication of fostering the literacy development of adults as well as children.

MULTIPLE PERSPECTIVES: TEACHERS, PARENTS, STUDENTS

The social framework of families as well as schools must be taken into account in discussing family literacy. In this section we highlight issues from the families' perspective, and also discuss the reciprocal influences on home-school relationships.

What we know now is that all parents want to be involved in their children's education. Minority, low-income, and non-English-speaking parents are equally as concerned as any other. However, families' ways of involvement may differ from those preferred by teachers, who may assume that parents who do not attend meetings at the school are uninterested in their children's education. Teachers may not know that parents are supporting their children's learning at home and they may not know how to build upon home support even when it is recognized. For example, storytelling, characteristic in many homes, could be used as a base for understanding the structure of written text, or a child's knowledge of the special vocabulary of a favorite sport or other home activity could be of help with word recognition skills.

Teachers' attitudes toward parents can be problematic; initial resistance to participating in parent programs is not uncommon. Demographic factors place demands on intercultural understanding; about 30% of the nation's schoolchildren are members of minority groups compared to only about 13% of the teaching force. However, attitudes are not fixed. With experience and with the appreciation from parents that has been seen to develop almost immediately, teachers develop a more positive stance (Epstein & Dauber, 1991).

For family members, factors inhibiting their involvement may be related to social class, minority status due to race or ethnicity, culture and language differences, or simply time pressures in households where all adults work outside the home (Finders & Lewis, 1994; U.S. Department of Education, 1994). For people in poverty, lack of transportation, lack of community support, and life stresses in the areas of health, personal safety, housing and basic economics often preclude adults' involvement in school functions. School events cannot be scheduled on days that welfare checks are due. A mother who must wait all day to be seen at a health clinic may need special incentives to attend a family literacy session at her child's school. A mother who had promised to help lead a session in a New Jersey program is robbed of the family's Christmas money by a drug-addicted relative and is too upset to come. Although the school expects that appointments will be kept and attendance at programs will be regular, the reality is that many adults miss appointments and have difficulty maintaining good attendance because of illness, frequent moves, and overwhelming family responsibilities (Morrow, 1995). In addition, since their own school experiences were frequently less than optimal, some adults may not be eager to walk through school gates once again.

Language and cultural practices may also be barriers. The parent whose English is limited may not be comfortable in school settings; using their more fluent children as interpreters may entail unwelcome reversals of authority, particularly among Asian populations (Puchner & Hardman, 1996). Teachers who speak their language, school communications written in the home language, the use of videos and other visual media, and English as a second language (ESL) classes at the school are suggestions for overcoming these barriers. It is worth emphasizing, also, that native English speakers can be confused by "educationese." All parents appreciate clear and jargon-free language.

In some cultures, education is considered the responsibility of the school, not the home, and families are surprised when they are asked to read to their children or learn methods for helping them with school subjects. Indeed, as Lareau (1989) points out, asking parents to take responsibility for cognitive learning, as distinct from responsibility for guiding their children's behavior, is a relatively new parental role. Although it is true that historically children were taught to read at home, that was probably confined to the affluent sector of society, and in any case a hands-off period of educational practice intervened until the 1960s.

Moll (1992), in a discussion of Latino parents, recommends that schools draw on the "funds of knowledge" in a community, using family members' expertise in their occupations or special skills as contributions to curriculum development, a recommendation applicable to family literacy programs as well. One of the joys in family literacy is the abundance of welcome revelations: finding out that a father is a writer of poetry that he agrees to share with the group, or that a grandmother has a fund of folk-tales, or that a mother has composed an African American version of *Goldilocks* for her children.

Although some parents may not recognize that they are a critical part of their child's education with regard to cognitive learning, it is common for many to say that they simply do not know how to help. In a study of inner-city schools in which teacher and parent perceptions were compared, Epstein (1991) found that whereas teachers reported that most parents were not involved with their children's education, parents "told a different story." They said that they were involved but needed more and better information from teachers about how to help at home. Similarly, Edwards (1995) in an interview study reported mothers' uncertainty about what reading to a child entailed. The low-literate African American mothers were aware of teachers' directive to read to their child but said that they did not know what to do in any specific sense or what books to read or, not being good readers themselves, how to do it correctly. Teachers, on the other hand, felt frustrated with the mothers' seeming lack of cooperation and wondered whether they cared if their children learned to read or not. Edwards then went on to build a program to help both groups, engaging mothers in a program of coaching, peer modeling, and parent-child interactions for book reading, and organizing a course for teachers to help them understand the multiple literacy environments of school and home.

Other cultural norms and expectations may differ. Although many programs are built on the assumption that the mother is the sole transmitter of literacy within the family, grandparents, fathers, other adult caretakers, and siblings may serve as "multiple channels of literacy influence" (Puchner & Hardman 1996). Durkin's (1966) study of early readers found that children commonly taught younger brothers and sisters to read, often within the context of playing school. In a discussion of Southeast Asian immigrants in the United States today, Puchner and Hardman (1996) describe sibling support as characteristic of these families; older children customarily help younger ones with their schoolwork.

Puchner and Hardman (1996) also highlight the different strategies that members of the immigrant culture have for helping their children succeed in school. Although poor English skills prevent parents for helping directly with schoolwork, they support learning in other ways, such as organizing household routines around homework activities, monitoring the homework, and offering incentives for good grades. Major implications of studies of Southeast Asian families are that literacy transfer between siblings is an important force and that English literacy transfer is more likely to go from child to adult, rather than the reverse (p. 3). A major implication for schools is the importance of knowledge about the home environments of the families.

MATCHES, MISMATCHES, AND RECIPROCAL RELATIONSHIPS

Matches and mismatches will affect classroom learning as well as influence the success of family literacy projects. A striking example of a match between the home of a working-class African American child and a mainstream school is provided in an autobiographical note by James P. Comer (1988), professor of child psychiatry and director of the School Development Program at Yale University's Child Study Center. He grew up in a stable, African American working-class family and attended a good elementary school in a largely White affluent community. Three friends, also African American and from apparently similar backgrounds, attended with him, but had very different life courses. Speculating why his life turned out better, Comer thinks that it was because his parents, unlike those of his friends, gave him "the social skills and confidence" that enabled him to take advantage of his educational opportunities. He said:

> My parents took me to the library so that I could read many books. My three friends, however, never read books—which frustrated and angered their teachers. What the teachers did not realize was that their parents were afraid to go to the library; indeed, they were uncomfortable around white people in general and avoided them. (pp. 42–43)

Comer also described how his mother consciously modeled her child rearing on middle-class White norms to enable her son to succeed in the majority culture. His experience is analogous to the stance of African American scholars Delpit (1995) and Edwards (1994), who argue that minority children should be taught the norms of mainstream schooling so that they may succeed academically and vocationally, rather than be limited to a culturally specific type of education.

In similar fashion, Comer's nationally acclaimed School Development Program addresses the "sociocultural misalignment problems of children from outside the mainstream" (Comer, 1988, p. 45) by instituting long-term plans for school reform that integrate home, school, and community services and bring the often discordant values of those institutions into alignment. Provided with consonant academic, social, developmental, and family services, children from minority groups are helped to achieve at their true level of ability.

Turning to a more specific level of cultural differences, home language socialization can have differing consequences for school achievement. As described by Heath (1983) in her comparative study of communities in the southeastern United States, children in a "mainstream" middle-class community who had much exposure to book reading and explanation as preschoolers did well in school because their home experience accorded with school culture. In a second community, children were trained to be passive and narrow readers of factual material; lacking active and elaborated habits of thought, they performed acceptably in early grades but could not sustain achievement later on in tasks of reading comprehension. A third community prized oral language; their children had developed highly creative oral-narrative abilities, but lacked understanding of the decontextualized nature of written text and of factual modalities such as labeling and categorizing. These children's poor performance in early school literacy tasks precluded opportunities to exercise their sophisticated narrative skills, and their subsequent school performance remained poor. Heath did not valorize any particular practice, but demonstrated the need for articulation between children's sociolinguistic experience at home and the practices of the school. She pointed out, for example, that the literacy of mainstream children might have benefited if narrative capabilities had been part of the classroom practice.

Cairney and Ruge (1996) also compared literacy behaviors in and out of school. In their case study of a mother and daughter, they compared three literacy environments of an Australian aboriginal family—home, school, and community Family Learning Center. The child reads and writes at the Family Learning Center, but not at school, where her teacher makes little attempt to involve her. During silent reading time, she "has a book on her desk, but does not read at all"—avoiding the activity, as in Purcell-Gates's (1995) study of an Appalachian boy who buried his face inside his desk during reading time. The school's assumption was that the lower-class, poorly performing child and mother had little interest in learning and no support of learning in the home. Emphasizing the "multiple worlds" in which the family lives, the researchers stressed the need for schools to be aware of that reality (p. 5).

Mismatches may be reciprocal, occurring on the part of families as well as schools. In the case of the Australian mother, she had assumed that if her child was not doing well, or if there was some problem, the school would contact her. Operating out of its own assumptions, the school did not. Of course these reciprocal assumptions worked to the detriment of the child. In the case of the Appalachian boy, Purcell-Gates (1995) demonstrates the confluence of factors that blocked this family's access to literacy. The wall of cultural stereotype and indifference constructed by a school that recognized only "mainstream" values was reinforced by the family's indifference to joining the mainstream as well as by its lack of familiarity with literate practices. In this study too an external organization, a university learning center, was the arena in which the family was developing its literacy.

Ethical issues are interwoven with the cultural mismatches and mistaken assumptions previously described. Cairney and Ruge (1996) put the matter succinctly:

> The initiators of any family literacy program immediately put themselves in a position of unequal power and hence begin to shape the agenda (no doubt unwittingly) to reflect their personal agendas. Since schools have typically been responsible for initiating most family and intergenerational programs, it is not surprising that many of these have been dominated by concerns with school literacy. (p. 2)

They suggest that schools must recognize the cultural practices of family and community and find ways in which to build effective communication.

Family literacy programs are designed to breach the home/school border; they implicate attitudes, behaviors, and interpersonal relations. Discussion of books and parenting may raise issues such as child rearing and discipline, upon which the values of educators and parents conflict. For instance parents sometimes casually mention hitting a restless child during book-reading. Although educators might readily suggest more productive ways to keep children interested, they must carefully and respectfully frame an issue where the parent perceived none. In a group setting, suggestions from other parents may be more welcome than those of the educator; sometimes, however, the group will voice solidarity with the proponent of physical punishment. It matters who does the counseling and how. In a family literacy session in an inner-city school, an older teacher was concerned about the lack of order in the children's home and its impact on their schoolwork. She told the young mothers about the importance of establishing routines for meals, homework, and bedtime; the young women were grateful: "Nobody ever told us that," they said. Here the personal authority of an older caring woman of their same ethnic background was accepted.

Other border-crossing issues include the families' use of time, making literacy important enough so that literacy plays a larger part in household activities. It is important also to have realistic expectations of the pace of change; families hard pressed by economic, health, or other life concerns may not be able to expend the time and effort that regular library trips involve, for example. Literacy development may also involve changing ways of discourse within the family. Whether such new practices as asking open-ended questions of a child or evoking a child's reaction to a story articulates with other values that parents might have or might be willing to develop is an open question. Another change that brings a positive response involves helping families become aware that many things routinely done in the home are literacy behaviors. Ranging from reading the Bible to writing a shopping list, those home practices can be used as foundational resources for further literacy development. Finally, there is the issue of cultural boundaries and the extent to which outsiders may participate. Telling another culture's story is a case in point. Storytellers in Native American cultures, for example, find it disturbing when non-Native schoolteachers want to tell their stories. How does one share another culture's story and which stories are heard?

There is now widespread recognition of the role of families in school learning. Despite the difficulties of turning recognition into practice, benefits accrue when schools are venues for family literacy programs. Schools gain the benefit of a wider understanding of the home context of their students. Family members coming to the school site learn about school and classroom operations, and will often serve as volunteers (Paratore, 1995). Parents will get to know teachers and, reciprocally, teachers will get to know parents. Learning will go both ways and facilitate two-way communication.

Unexpected things happen in schools. The secretary in a New Jersey school that had recently begun a family literacy program, kept a children's book on her desk and would use her 15-minute break to run into classrooms and read to the children. Somehow, she also managed time away from her desk to attend the family literacy workshops for parents. Asked about her interest, she said:

> Parents need to pay attention to their children. One day my daughter (a first grader) said to me "Mommy, I'm going to read this book to you" and it shocked me. This was my child and I didn't know she could read. I was so proud, so happy. Then when they started this program in the school, I wanted to be part of it, part of my child's education.

After an initial mismatch, the failure of school and parent to communicate about a child's progress, the availability of a family literacy program at the school helped this working mother foster her child's literacy development and she in turn helped the school by becoming a reading model for many of its students.

CHAPTER 4

The Partnership for Family Reading

We can't come out after dark.

It will never work here.

Where can I find books in Spanish?

Why doesn't my school have this program?

I learn as much as my child.

THOSE ARE THE VOICES of teachers, parents, and administrators in the Partnership for Family Reading, an intergenerational literacy program between Montclair State University and the Newark, New Jersey, public schools that has been active for 8 years. Newark is the largest city in the state and one of the most troubled in terms of urban problems and ineffective schools. Montclair State University, 10 miles distant in a pleasant town, had worked with the school district in various ways for many years in fulfillment of its commitment to urban schools. The Partnership for Family Reading was its first venture into the field of family literacy. The Partnership's aim was twofold: to foster the literacy development of adult family members and their children and to help elementary school staff function as family literacy educators.

It was my mission to help address those challenges, together with the educators with whom I worked. Their orientation was toward helping children; the other purposes of the Partnership were endorsed more gradually as our work proceeded. In adopting those aims, the Partnership set about consciously to bring change to the school district. The district had had no prior family literacy program, the concept of intergenerational learning was new, and, as in most districts, teachers were not prepared to be family educators. Further, the literacy model used by the Partnership brought

41

change. Fostering reading through engagement with interesting children's books and interactive strategies, its program contrasted with the skills-based curriculum then in use in Newark schools.

Previously we have explored characteristics of family literacy and some of the issues and challenges associated with the field. The focus of this chapter spotlights one program in a specific school district to illuminate those themes further. I will also take a reflective look at the program from the perspective of 8 years, sharing my own perspectives as well as representing those of others as I understand them.

The Newark program was designated a partnership to emphasize the collaboration between the university, school district, administrators, teachers, and family members. As director, I believed that the Partnership should benefit all of the stakeholders, family members and teachers alike. The major activity of the Partnership was a series of workshops for adult family members in which they learned generic reading strategies used by good readers as they read and discussed interesting children's literature. They then participated in reading sessions with their children transmitting what they had learned and learning about their children's interests and reading behaviors in the process. The aim was literacy development of both generations.

Partnership for Family Reading activities began in one school in 1987 and grew to a membership of 34 schools serving about 2,000 families over a period of 8 years; Family Reading is now institutionalized in some ten schools that are continuing the program without direct involvement on the part of the university. Activities are targeted to families with children in kindergarten through Grade 3; in some cases, families with preschoolers and older children attended as well. A total of 90 educators participated in staff development and conducted family workshops. Participating family members were predominantly female—mothers, grandmothers, and aunts; perhaps one percent of the family participants were male—fathers, grandfathers, older brothers, and an occasional husband who attended with his wife.

The Partnership workshops followed a model called Family Reading (Goldsmith & Handel, 1990). In order to illuminate the adult literacy perspective that was its origin, I will give a bit of its history.

LISTENING TO THE LEARNERS

The model for the Partnership workshops evolved from a prior program at a community college. In 1985, I was teaching developmental reading to adult students at New York City Technical College, a unit of the City University of New York. Students had been assigned to the course because they had failed the college reading test. This was my first full-time academic position and I was eager to find my way in new territory. My students' ages ranged from 18 to 50, with most being in their late 20s and 30s. First in their families to go to college, they were low-income people representing many nationalities and ethnic groups. They held down jobs while going to school; a large number were parents as well.

Both the students and I found the prescribed developmental curriculum unsatisfactory. Many students were passive and uninvolved during the class sessions. After class, however, they would cluster around to ask questions. What they asked was how they could help their children. What was my opinion of a certain children's book or what books could I recommend for them to read aloud? Could I help them find information on child development? They asked about schoolwork and where materials on school topics could be found. What advice could I give them about certain school practices their children were facing?

Listening to my students, I became aware of their deep concern for their children's welfare. I was struck, also, by the difference between their relative passivity toward their prescribed remedial work and their activist interest in their children. Eventually, I synthesized my observations. The need of my students to learn how to improve their own reading and their heartfelt desire to help their children might come together in ways that could serve both purposes.

From that insight, workshops for students who were caretakers of young children evolved as a colleague and I developed the program. As described by Handel and Goldsmith (1988, 1989), we built on the students' motivation and introduced them to exciting children's books. We modeled reading strategies, such as questioning and predicting, that are used by learners of all ages, engaged them in peer learning and in group discussion of the relationships of the books to their own lives and to broader themes of interest. We helped them select books for home reading with their children. Adult selections coordinated with the topics of the children's books were also read. Each semester, children and adults participated in a family reading celebration at the college. From these early experiences, we developed the first published family literacy curriculum (Goldsmith & Handel, 1990) detailing the workshop activities and their rationale.

THE NEWARK CONTEXT

The Family Reading model was designed to be flexible and has been adapted to the various settings in which it is in use, as the description of Reading Starts with Us (see Chapter 2) illustrates. Elsewhere, in San Diego, California, it proved adaptable to a state mandate for parent involvement;

in Rochester, New York, where another family program, Family Math, was already in place, Family Reading was absorbed into the district's after-school structure with parents and students attending the program together.

In 1988, I brought Family Reading to the Newark, New Jersey, public schools in conjunction with Montclair State University, where I was now teaching. My first task was to become as familiar as possible with this new environment. Newark, with a population somewhat over 275,000, is the largest city in New Jersey. Subject to a daunting list of urban ills, it has an unemployment rate of 12.6% or twice the state average, a median family income of $12,000, a sizable homeless population, and one third of the residents on welfare. According to the 1990 census, the city's racial and ethnic breakdown is 63% non-Hispanic Black; 26% Hispanic (may be any race); 10% non-Hispanic White; and about 1% Asian. The Newark School District enrolls 47,000 students in its 80 schools. Parent involvement was a district goal, but few structures for implementation existed. Despite above-average per-pupil spending, student performance was poor; drop-out rates averaged 50%; and less than half of the high school students pass proficiency tests in reading and math. In 1995, the state took over the school district for the district's failure to discharge its obligations to students. Rather than working as a member of a relatively cohesive institution, I was now an outsider working with a troubled citywide school district with many schools and competing interests.

There were other challenges. Although I worked directly with family members at the outset, it was clear that teachers were to be the facilitators of the program. They had the day-to-day contact with parents and their participation would be the means of insuring that the program was institutionalized in the school. Staff development was needed; at the time, the district had little record of involving parents in the school and few teachers were encouraged or trained in doing so. Accordingly, as modified for the schools, the Family Reading model would have to address two distinct groups of adults, teachers as well as family members of the children, and the participants for both groups would have to be recruited. Finally, instead of being an integral part of the institution where these changes were to occur, I was an external agent, who needed to establish bona fides and to prove the usefulness of what I was advocating. Previous experience of family members' concern for their children's literacy development convinced me that Newark parents would feel the same. As so many researchers have demonstrated, that was indeed the case. Low-income, minority parents were concerned for their children's welfare and wanted to help. But many wondered how.

THE FAMILY READING MODEL

The Family Reading workshop model draws on several strands of literacy research. It is a holistic model that regards literacy development as a recursive, rather than linear, process, and one that includes the exercise of phonic skills, oral storytelling, text creation, and critical thinking. Learners receive instruction in cognitive strategies, such as accessing prior knowledge, making predictions and other types of inferences, generating questions, and relating text to other text and to personal experience, as entry points into comprehending the children's books, not as isolated skills. In accordance with constructivist views of literacy learning and adult education principles that honor learners' experience and knowledge, learners are viewed as "active participants in the creation of their own knowledge" as mediated by their prior experiences and purposes (Hiebert, 1991, p. 2). Thus there are many opportunities for participation and few "right" answers built into the model. Rather, the focus is on stimulating thought and wide-ranging discussion, including discussion of abstract issues suggested by the children's books. In emphasizing discussion of this type, the model follows the work of Snow, Barnes, Chandler, Goodman, and Hemphill (1991), which maintains that abstract or noncontextualized discourse promotes high levels of literacy.

Family Reading is also a model that endorses enjoyment as a condition for adult learning. Following theories of intrinsic motivation (Csikszentmihalyi, 1990), enjoyment was considered an important factor in transmitting reading experiences to others and sustaining learnings over time. Family Reading establishes a social context for adult learning, the informal workshop group in which individual meaning construction is shared and reinterpreted through interaction with others. The sociable nature of the workshops and the enjoyable children's books were intended to strengthen enthusiasm for reading and to provide a positive learning environment. Children's literature seemed the natural medium in which the reciprocal influences of affect and cognition could flourish. The model attempted to link those two domains.

The Family Reading workshops for adult family members were experiential and participatory, designed for a high degree of dialogue and discussion stimulated by reading children's books. There were no "right" or "wrong" answers; rather the focus was on active engagement and exchange of ideas. Children's literature was the material of choice because of its benefits to adult readers in terms of accessibility and adaptability to inquiry learning (see also Bloem & Padak, 1996), but also because of its enjoyable qualities. In fact, participants were uniformly delighted with the children's books, most of which were new to them. The integration of cognitive reading strategies into the reading of children's books distinguished the model from programs that focus on book reading alone.

Snow and Tabors (1996) discuss enjoyment and engagement as a mechanism for intergenerational transfer that might help explain individual differences among children. Presumably, positive affect around books, including individual attention from parents who find reading a source of enjoyment and enjoy reading to their children, helps children persist in the acquisition of beginning reading skills; later their expectation of enjoyment "leads to more time spent reading, i.e. more practice, and thus greater fluency—a major predictor of long-term reading outcomes" (p. 76). Engagement and enjoyment may be particularly important for children from disadvantaged groups, who have less reason to believe that literacy will serve them as a route to school or occupational success. Enjoyment—a neglected variable in much educational planning—is a powerful source of intrinsic motivation that is linked to cognitive development. Family Reading workshops that were enjoyable as well as instructive were intended to help adults develop the knowledge and strengthen the disposition to foster literacy for their children and themselves.

The reading sessions of adults with children were guided by Vygotsky's (1978) theories of adult mediation of children's learning, in which the more expert adult thinks aloud, models strategies, or offers supportive clues as a means of helping young readers incorporate those ways of thinking into their own internal repertoire. Since feelings as well as cognitions would be transmitted in the social interaction with children, the adults' positive response in their workshops was particularly important. Research showing cognitive gains for tutors as well as for those being helped also provided rationale for the adult-child book-reading aspect of the model. Finally, in terms of Nickse's (1990) family literacy typology, the Family Reading model provided direct services to adults and indirect services to children.

The workshop model was structured as follows:

1. Introductory activities
2. Introduction of the children's book and the genre represented
3. Modeling of a reading strategy using the children's book
4. Practice in pairs
5. Discussion
6. Preparation for reading to children

FAMILY READING WORKSHOP SESSIONS

At the first workshop of the year, participants were asked to think back to their own childhoods and share memories of reading, storytelling, writing, or books. They were asked to remember who was involved in the early experience, where it occurred, and how they had felt. This activity, intended to reintroduce participants into the literacy arena and to help develop group cohesion, engaged them in recollection that was usually positive, sometimes poignant, occasionally humorous, and always interesting to other members of the group. It also prepared the way for the next step, presentation of a children's book representing a particular genre. Comments about the genre were then solicited from the participants in order to make connections with their knowledge and interests. For example, if the genre was folktales, the parents and workshop facilitator recounted tales that they remembered, often reflecting their different ethnic backgrounds. If an informational book was to be used, participants would discuss sources of everyday information and share interesting items. Poetry would evoke familiar rhymes and in several cases uncover the revelation that a participant or someone she knew wrote poetry. The books selected were mainly picture books; attention was directed to deriving meaning from the illustrations and to the relationship of picture to text. Wordless picture books were also used to foster oral language and narrative.

Next, the workshop facilitator modeled reading strategies in a holistic way while reading parts of the children's book aloud. Listening to a model of fluent, expressive reading, the group would also respond to such strategies as making predictions, generating questions, accessing background knowledge, and relating personal experience to the text. Then the adults paired up to read the book aloud to one another while practicing the strategies. This was the time in the workshop when everyone smiled, enjoying both the reading and the sociability of sharing with another adult.

The fifth step, group discussion, began with the workshop facilitator asking for feedback on the strategy that had just been practiced; what predictions had been made? what questions generated? Next the discussion would proceed on a higher level to a critique of the book based on the participants' own experiences and values. Then, on the highest level of generalization, the more abstract issues suggested by the book would be discussed. It was the workshop facilitator's role to help the discussion along by raising issues, sharing impressions, and covering the three levels of discussion. The discussions were more often recursive than strictly sequential. No two were ever alike.

The multicultural, quality children's literature, selected for its interest to adults as well as children, served as a springboard for consideration of important issues often related to child rearing and human relations. For example, the fable *The Lion and the Mouse* provided an occasion to make analogies to what even small children can do and the importance of recognizing their contributions. *Stevie*, by John Steptoe, dealt with sibling jealousy. Vera B. Williams's *A Chair for My Mother* stimulated discussions of single motherhood, family cooperation, and the importance of thrift (opinions differed). Nonfiction tradebooks were also included to help provide an expanded knowledge and the opportunity for explanation that expository texts are likely to elicit. *Bread Bread Bread*, a book of photographs by Ann Morris, gave information about customs and types of bread in different parts of the world and prompted learners to explore grocery shelves for ethnic products that were new to them. The folktale *The Little Red Hen* resonated with many hardworking mothers; some decided to read the story to their own "lazy" families in an effort to make them shape up. One woman said: "I am like that hen; I do all the work around the house and get no thanks." There was energetic discussion of the morality of the hen's refusal to share food with the lazy friends. Several mothers agreed that the hen should have warned them ahead of time about what would happen if they didn't cooperate; others disagreed. Several alternate endings for the story were proposed. Thus, the strategies and discussion engaged participants in relating text to life and life to text, and in some cases in creating alternate texts.

Children's literature, particularly narrative, was especially powerful in fostering insight and openness to change. Narrative engages feelings, presents an organized chain of events, and does not make the reader as uncomfortable or resistant as teaching by overt precept might. It permits readers to distance themselves and reflect on meaning when dealing with issues that are personally or culturally sensitive. For example, participants were delighted to discuss a story about a child of an interracial marriage who observed both Asian and Western customs, and wanted to try Japanese food and eat with chopsticks.

For many, the workshops represented their first experience in discussing books with others in a nonthreatening atmosphere in which diversity of meaning was welcome. Similarly, Goldsmith (1995) showed how family literacy programs can support change through the development of tolerance for different points of view; Neuman, Celano, and Fischer (1996) also described how adolescent mothers connected literacy to real-life concerns and goals when discussing multicultural children's books.

The final workshop component, preparation for reading to children, involved adults in discussing how they would present the book to their child and what their child's reaction was likely to be. After each workshop, the adults borrowed the books and shared their enjoyment and learning with their children; the book reading occurred both at home and in school classrooms. In the case of the latter, children greeted their parents eagerly and became absorbed in reading together.

At the beginning of the following workshop session, home-reading experiences were shared. This sharing was another opportunity for group cohesion. Mothers said they had learned new things about their children's

abilities and interests as a result of discussing books with them and expressed pride in the children's curiosity. They commented on how their
older children tended to gather round at book-reading time, making Family
Reading an activity for the entire family. They shared advice on how to
keep a restless child interested, warning against scheduling reading too
close to the time of a favorite TV show. Sometimes they reported that their
children wanted to hear the book straight through without stopping for
questions or discussion, but on a subsequent rereading liked to respond to
the interactive strategies. Participants compared notes and learned together.
After this introductory activity, a new book was introduced and the cycle
of book presentation, strategy modeling, peer practice, group discussion,
and preparation for reading to children began again.

Schools held five or six workshops per year, followed by a recognition
ceremony. The activities were facilitated by school staff who had received
staff development in the Family Reading model, which they experienced in
much the same manner as did the family groups. Refreshments were available at every session and the atmosphere was one of informality and welcome. Some schools provided child care; at others, preschoolers accompanied their parents to the workshops and participated in the book reading.

To engage the participation of the various cultural groups in Newark,
sessions were conducted in Spanish as well as English; translators were
provided for speakers of Asian languages and Portuguese. Teachers who
were native Spanish speakers conducted the Spanish sessions. In some
schools, dual sessions in English and Spanish went on simultaneously with
the two groups socializing before and after. Children's books that were
published in both English and Spanish versions were provided; in some
cases books were translated. Participants who read Spanish books in the
workshops often wanted to take the English version home so they could
practice their English using material that was now familiar to them. Some
Spanish speakers, becoming adept in the new language, preferred attending
workshops in English. Others who stayed with the Spanish were assured
that children would benefit regardless of the language in which parents
read to them. Participants spoke of the help their children gave them with
their greater English-language facility, an example of literacy transmission
from child to parent that is portrayed in the children's book *I Speak English for My Mom.*

The Family Reading model used in Newark was guided by pragmatics
as well as research. The workshops were sufficiently structured so that
participants felt they had learned something that they were then able to
put it into practice. But there was also flexibility and much opportunity for
them to contribute. For the workshop facilitators, the strategies served as
accessible instructional routines, giving them a teaching mode with which
they were familiar. The structured nature of the workshops was also delib-

erate, keyed to the needs of the district. Because teachers in the district had so little experience working with parents and there were so many logistical obstacles to overcome, it seemed realistic to offer them a project rather than ask them to create one at least initially. Very quickly, of course, the workshops broadened out as teachers adapted the structure and introduced new features as needs arose in their schools, a process discussed in more detail in Chapter 9.

The characteristics of the Family Reading model that distinguished it from family literacy programs that do not address adult learning are the practice-with-peers component, to reinforce the learning of interactive strategies, and the adult-level discussion of issues raised by the children's literature. To encourage further application of the reading strategies, adult selections that paralleled the theme of the children's books were also available at the workshops. Both the strategy learning and the discussions were intended to engage participants in what has been called decontextualized talk (Snow & Tabors, 1996), that is, talk that goes beyond the immediate here and now, or, in the case of reading, beyond the literal context of the book. Making associations, analyzing, explaining, asking "why" questions, and interpreting motives and feelings are examples of nonimmediate talk that research suggests are related to cognitive outcomes that foster reading achievement and higher level comprehension in particular (Snow et al., 1991). The intent was to give participants experience in developing those levels of thought. The assumption was not that participants were unfamiliar with the cognitive strategies, but to demonstrate, encourage, and explore the possibilities of applying them in book talk with their children and in book reading for themselves.

Parental reading to children has been widely regarded as the single most important factor in early reading achievement (Anderson et al., 1985), providing knowledge about the conventions of written text as well as vocabulary development and motivation to read. Book reading and establishing an enjoyable reading relationship with children were at the heart of the Family Reading experience, but the reading was to include strategies and discussion in order to foster a broader understanding of literacy. Also, guided by the importance of engagement in literacy practices as a means of literacy improvement, Family Reading encouraged library visits as well as home reading, provided books as resources, and encouraged parents to model literacy for their children as a practice useful to adults.

PROGRAM IMPLEMENTATION

The Partnership was designed as a school-based program and, as might be expected, implementation varied across the school sites. Although all the

34 schools followed the Family Reading model, differences in staff expertise, administrative support, resources, and receptivity of parents to the
new venture accounted for the variations in program operation. Site diversity was taken into account from the beginning on the understanding that
certain aspects of the program would be shaped by it. In some schools, for
example, there was no time for parents to read to their children in the
school building. In others, parents read in classrooms or, in schools that
could accommodate a different type of organization, children came out of
classrooms to meet their parents in a central facility. In several schools in
which parents went into classrooms at the conclusion of the adult workshop, they read to small groups, not just to their individual child, so that
children who did not have family members in attendance would not be left
out. Those parents were seen to exhibit special competencies in their book
holding and questioning behavior, modeling themselves on what they had
seen teachers do in workshop demonstrations and reporting pride in the
accomplishment of being able to engage the attention of a group of youngsters.

Some schools limited the program to kindergarten families; others
found it feasible to extend it through Grade 3. Several principals evaluated
success in terms of number of participants only, and did not provide resources to support program quality. At a few sites, the culture of the school
supported parent involvement; there Family Reading was incorporated as
a natural addition to projects. At most others, Family Reading was the
pioneer effort to reach out to parents and the cornerstone on which other
family projects were built. Through external and internal grants, the Partnership supplied all schools with workshop books. As director, I was also
instrumental in persuading schools to open their school libraries to parent
book borrowing. Nonetheless, differences in such basic resources as rooms
in which to hold the workshops, funds to pay for refreshments, and time
for teachers to plan the sessions still existed. Staff exercised much ingenuity
to overcome these logistical obstacles. To the greatest extent possible, unrealistic demands upon resources and staff were avoided. A negative aspect
was a lack of uniformity, which made program management and evaluation more difficult.

The Partnership went through three phases over its 8 years: initiation,
implementation, and institutionalization. However, since schools joined the
Partnership in successive waves, each school was on its own timetable.
Experience with the earlier joining schools benefited those that joined later.

The Partnership grew gradually from the bottom up. It began in one
school with the one teacher who was interested in working with parents. I
had hoped for more and that eventually her colleagues would join in, but
in the spring of 1987 it was just this one adventurous teacher who issued
invitations to parents and together with me shared children's books with

them in the kindergarten classroom. During a summer conference, she spread the word, and subsequently teachers from two other schools expressed interest, sparked by her enthusiasm.

Awareness of the program spread through both formal and informal means. An important formal factor in extending the Partnership to additional schools was an organization of Newark administrators with whom I met for the purpose of addressing issues of school improvement. As the university coordinator, I had some influence over the agenda, and, when I showed slides of parent workshops, additional principals, including those who had shown little interest before, demanded that their schools be included. By the end of the year, seven schools were participating in the Partnership. Teams of teachers from each of the schools were identified; I met with them, in monthly staff development sessions, and observed or participated in parent workshops at the schools. Family Reading festivals and a conference on families and schools were held on campus. The Newark central office assigned administrators to collaborate in Partnership management and began to promote the Partnership to all elementary schools in the district. When some years later the District shifted from a skill-and-drill reading curriculum to one that was more literature based, that also helped validate the Family Reading workshops.

As a result of district endorsement and teacher word of mouth, the number of Partnership schools gradually grew to 34. As numbers increased, my personal involvement in individual schools became less intense. Staff development sessions were now held on campus; teams from new schools met for a 2-day session in the fall and a one-day follow-up in late spring at which they reported on their first-year programs and shared ideas. Yearly staff development was offered to the experienced teams as well; they developed new workshop units, evaluated new children's books, and in some cases shared in the training of the newly formed teams. Despite many personnel and organizational changes, at this time Family Reading is well institutionalized and operating without university support in at least 10 schools.

Funding and staff to work with all of the 34 schools did not keep pace with the rapid growth of the Partnership. Spurred by the school district and enthusiastic teachers, the project simply outgrew its resources as additional schools participated. As a result, the Partnership remained rather narrowly focused and often did not coordinate with other school reform efforts in the district. However, as the years progressed, the district promoted family involvement more vigorously and many schools included Family Reading in their school improvement plans (for more details, see Handel, 1990b).

CHAPTER 5

The Women of Family Reading

> It is the design of this volume . . . to assist the
> mother in her efforts to interest her child in
> learning to read, and to aid her in promoting
> its progress in that very serious, and, indeed,
> formidable undertaking.
> —Jacob Abbott, *Learning to Read*

Learning to Read, a book found on a dusty shelf in a secondhand shop, is one of many published during the mid-19th century, a period that emphasized moral education in the home and the key role of mothers as home teachers. Basic literacy was the mother's job, and reading was a "formidable" task that began with letter recognition. The book consists of informational excerpts and short moral tales that the mother was to read aloud while pointing out the letters and asking questions about the pictures. Reading was a skill learned through repetition and recognition, and the mother's role was a didactic one. Today we hear that parents (usually meaning mothers) are their children's first teacher, and, although concepts of literacy may have broadened, many people still consider basic skills the most important component of literacy that they can teach to children.

In many family literacy programs, as in the Partnership for Family Reading, the great majority of participants are women—the mothers, grandmothers, aunts, or other female caretakers of the children involved—but programs typically refer to them as "parents" or "family members" and do not publicly identify their gender. In neglecting to do so, those programs may fail to take account of the distinctive needs, interests, abilities, or personal history of the women involved. Similarly, the vast majority of elementary school teachers and educators who lead family literacy programs are women. That fact too often goes unrecognized. To counter that trend, the perspectives of mothers and teachers who participated in the Partnership for Family Reading will be foregrounded in this section and the meaning of participation to these women will be explored.

In taking a phenomenological stance (Lincoln & Guba, 1985), or in exploring the program's meaning from the standpoint of the adult participants, I attempt to represent their felt experience. Beyond the acknowledgment that parents and teachers wish to foster children's development, few studies explore the meaning of their involvement in family literacy programs. The goal here is to represent women whose voices are often not heard, explore the meanings that their participation holds for them, and suggest ways that women have benefited from the family literacy effort. Seen through the researcher's lens—that less than transparent instrument— the participants' felt experience is considered a source of knowledge. The resulting portrayals, although necessarily incomplete, suggest the variety of meanings that participation in Family Reading has evoked.

Exploring the perspective of participants is part of the learner-centered approach to program evaluation, teaching, and learning advocated by many literacy researchers (Auerbach, 1989; Lytle, Belzer, & Reumann, 1992; Weinstein-Shr, 1990; Wikelund, 1993, among others). Teacher research has found educators' beliefs, values, and personal experience to be influential in the practice of their profession. The perspective of the parents served is an important "but often neglected" aspect of family intervention programs, according to Scott-Jones (1992), who questions the appropriateness of programs that do not acknowledge parents as authorities on their own children; in addition, she advocates special attention to the needs and characteristics of minority families. More generally, social scientists engaged in crafting feminist theory, methodology, and practice in a wide variety of research arenas insist on the subjectivity of all parties to the research process, including that of researchers (Reinharz, 1992). Clearly, too, the personal meanings and motivations of key adults at home and school are particularly important because of their impact on children's literacy learning.

Feminist researchers and others perceive the interconnectedness of women's lives. In the adult literacy field it is commonly acknowledged that a frequent motivation for embarking on a literacy program is a parent's wish to be able to help children with homework or to read to them. Ripple effects on home life have been seen even from workplace literacy programs focused on specific job-related skills. On the other hand, household responsibilities, opposition from family members, and the lack of such resources as child care or transportation may affect women's participation in a negative way.

In seeking to enhance the literacy of both generations, family literacy programs are well situated to strengthen linkages between school and home literacy contexts. The home visitor component of the federal Even Start program is a step in that direction. In general, however, institutional and class boundaries mean that the home context is less well known to literacy providers, particularly those affiliated with schools, and that the perspective of literacy learners on possible linkages and connections is often not systematically sought. Similarly, too, the home contexts of literacy providers are often unknown to the adult learners, and the teachers may not themselves make connections between their personal and professional lives, or between their personal lives and those of their adult learners.

In seeking to cross those boundaries through the participatory and constructivist model adopted by the Family Reading Partnership, teachers, parents, and I shared experiences and ideas as family members and as learners. We exchanged memories of our early literacy experiences and of our lives with our own children; we collaborated on program design, reflected on our learning, and exchanged views about the books we read.

As the individuality of the participating mothers came into focus in the Family Reading workshops, and as the enthusiasm of the teachers grew, it became clear that participation in the program was sustained by a variety of reasons. What accounted for their sustained interest? What, from their standpoint, were the benefits, limitations, misunderstandings, and unintended consequences of their participation? In what ways did the program articulate with their personal history and their out-of-school lives? How might gender, ethnicity, and social class influence their participation? What were the connections to the school and school instruction? And what lessons could be derived for family literacy practice and for the larger context of literacy research? These questions guided the exploration of learners' and teachers' perspectives.

MOTHERS' RESPONSES TO THE FAMILY READING WORKSHOPS

Over the 8 years of the Partnership, participants were asked what changes in their literacy practices might have occurred as a result of attending Family Reading. Surveys conducted in the schools were supplemented by observations of Family Reading workshops and group interviews with family members and teachers. Formal literacy testing of the adults was not feasible.

This data showed that the predominantly female family members were functioning in three important and interrelated ways: as literacy learners; as literacy resources for their children; and as actors in the world with regard to literacy (Handel & Goldsmith, 1994).

LITERACY LEARNERS

The mothers reported that the Family Reading workshops helped promote their own adult development in literacy, that their interest and competencies in reading had improved. They were reading more, applying reading strategies to what they read, and borrowing books on topics of interest. Resumption was a common theme; Family Reading was seen as a continuation of their education—a second chance "now that I'm older and know better," as one high school dropout remarked—and as a stimulus to pick up a book again, something that many had not done since high school. Typical was one mother's reflection:

> I used to read, then stopped after school. Now I go to someone's house, see a book, and I think this looks like a good book to read.

Although many of the parents had known that reading to a child was important, they had not known where its importance lay or how and when to carry this out. A typical comment was,

> Before I thought reading was just reading. Now I know it's also talking and asking questions.

The common assumption that reading was oral performance for a silent listener had given way to an enlarged concept of literacy as social interaction. That was a major understanding that Family Reading promoted through the interactive workshops. Overall, the women expressed more understanding of their role as home educator; perhaps now they felt that they had more to give.

LITERACY RESOURCES

As literacy resources, mothers were bringing more books into the home and, through the strategic reading and discussion with their children, were enhancing the quality of the experience as well. They reported taking children on library trips and getting library cards. In addition, as a result of reading to their children in a more interactive way, they were creating enjoyable reading relationships and strengthening bonds by learning more about their children, taking pride in their personal traits ("I never realized my child was so curious") and attending to their interests. The adults' function as reading role models by virtue of their increased orientation to books and their participation in the Family Reading workshops was also part of their sharpened role as literacy resource. Not incidentally, the children were delighted to see their parents in school; the postworkshop reading sessions were a special joy for both. Teachers observed that the children were more interested in classroom reading as a result of parental reading at home and school. Significantly, too, participants had developed new understandings of the educational role of parents. "I learned that I must continue to be an active partner in my child's reading program" and "I learned that working with your children helps a lot with their education" were typical comments.

ACTORS IN THE WORLD

As actors in the world, many women were bringing literacy to bear on personal and social goals. They were teaching friends and relatives Family Reading strategies and sharing books; some read to neighbors' children; some encouraged other mothers to participate in the school workshops; others started the program in their church. One grandmother brought the program to her numerous grandchildren. "It's a family program; everybody is supposed to read," she said, describing a household in which three generations—grandmother, mothers, and all the children down to the newest baby—were engaged with books. Some parents reported plans to get their high school equivalency diplomas; several served as school aides; one organized a parents' resource room in the school. In Freirean terms, the word was beginning to reach out to the world.

MOTIVATIONS

Beyond those responses closely associated with literacy, interpersonal motivations were at work in participants' responses to Family Reading. Foremost was the welcoming atmosphere of the Family Reading workshops. The welcome by the school and by the teacher facilitators was a major initial motivation. Participants felt comfortable in the school. They liked the "good news" aspect of the program, being in the school to do something interesting rather than being called in only when there was a problem. They responded to their children's enthusiastic invitations. They felt particularly gratified when the principal or other especially important people joined the workshop and read a favorite book. Some women also came because it was a chance to get out of the house. "I don't have many friends," one mother said; "I come for the sociability." Some women came for the food, particularly if a light lunch was served. On winter days several to whom I spoke came because their apartment was unheated and the school was warm. It was important to recognize and provide for these diverse aspects when planning the program. Overall, the enjoyable and informal nature of the Family Reading workshops helped in recruiting and retaining participants and in so doing played a large part in promoting the outcomes of literacy learner, literacy resource, and actor in the world.

A second important factor was at work as well, articulation with a central value that the participants held. Consistently throughout, participants talked of how the program promoted family togetherness. Their reports of how the home-reading activity had brought parents and children together indicated the high value that participants placed on that outcome. Typical comments were,

We became closer.

It creates family togetherness because we all sit down and read to everyone.

We read together as a family. We have more to talk about and enjoy.

The home reading and the conversation that it entailed served as a vehicle for increased family closeness. That appeared in turn to have strengthened the family members' continued participation in the program through establishing a mutually reinforcing cycle of involvement between home and school activities. Consonant with the program's promotion of enjoyment as a factor in cognitive learning during the workshops, enjoyable reading relationships had carried over into the home. Articulation with participants' value system is an important part of any educational program. For these women, the special value of literacy lay in its effect on their family relations. Added to the several possible uses of reading—entertainment, information, affirmation of belief, skill building—was the social-interactional one of fostering family cohesion.

INTERVIEWING THE MOTHERS

Responses to the surveys and group observations stimulated more questions. Are the parents getting anything else out of the program? What else might participation mean to them? What home environments do they come from and what do they bring back to their home environment? What else might be learned that could be helpful in school-home relationships? To explore those questions, I interviewed seven mothers who had consistently attended Family Reading workshops at a well-established program in one school.

The ages of the women interviewed ranged from 24 to 43. All have lived in Newark since childhood; two are graduates of the school now attended by their children. Five of the women had high school diplomas or the equivalent, one had completed Grade 11, and one mother, a contrast case, had an advanced academic degree. Overall, their educational level was higher than average for their community. All of the women interviewed were African American, as were more than 95% of the children and about 50% of the staff at the school in question, called here Central School. Table 5.1 presents selected demographic information. To protect privacy, all names are pseudonyms.

Four of the mothers had children in kindergarten and had attended all five Family Reading workshops during the interview year. One mother had a child in first grade and was completing 2 years of attendance; and two mothers of third graders were completing their 4th year with the program, having participated since their children were in kindergarten. Together, the study participants form a core of "regulars" at the school's Family Reading workshops.

Central School, located in one of the most impoverished and crime-ridden areas of Newark, has participated in the Partnership since the fall of 1987, and continues to participate. Firmly institutionalized, Central School now draws 25–35 family members to its workshops sessions, the best attended in the district. The program's success is due largely to the leadership and commitment of the key Family Reading facilitator, Ms. Conti, an experienced kindergarten teacher who adopted the program soon after its inception in the district and has added many distinctive features of her own to the Family Reading model, such as a yearlong focus on critical thinking or on a spectrum of multicultural books, and on storybooks that featured mathematics concepts. As parents became more familiar with each of the reading strategies, she shifted to a more natural way of using them, and, rather than focusing on just one strategy during book reading, modeled the flexible use of several different ones.

Ms. Conti has also added critical analysis of illustrations and manipulative activities, such as reading games and make-and-take activities to the workshop program. She sends home a small newsletter, exhorts students to encourage their parents to attend, and uses door prizes as incentives. At the end of each year, students perform for their parents and see them recognized and awarded a certificate by the school. The workshops are held in the school library, from which parents may borrow books. A table of refreshments is always provided.

A White woman of Italian heritage, Ms. Conti is known for her welcoming manner with parents. Family members are often seen visiting her classroom or chatting with her in the hall. As a teacher, she runs a well-

Table 5.1. Respondents—Selected Demographics

	Age	Education	Occupational History	Others in Household
Marge Burns	24	H.S. grad.	(Former) food handler	Son, age 5, kindergarten Son, 17 mos. Mother
Alicia Smiley	29	H.S. grad. + business school	(Former) secretary	Son, age 5, kindergarten Son, age 16 mos.
Ann Powers	38	H.S. grad.	—	Daughter, age 5, kindergarten Son, age 14, 8th grade Daughter, age 18, 11th grade Son, age 20, H.S. grad. Niece, age 3 Nephew, age 11, 5th grade
Mercedes Smith	43	J.D.	Attorney	Daughter, age 5, kindergarten Son, age 10, 5th grade Husband
Linda Green	24	Grade 11	(Former) cafeteria aide	Daughter, age 6, 1st grade Sons, age 4 ½ & 2 ½, in preschool Mother Two sisters
Sue Afton	29	H.S. grad.	Aide, institution for mentally disabled	Daughter, age 8, 3rd grade Husband
Harriet Blank	42	GED	—	Daughter, age 8, 3rd grade Son, age 8, 3rd grade Son, age 24, H.S. grad. Children's father

Note: All respondents are African American. Names have been changed.

organized kindergarten and has high expectations of her students; parents say that their children "love" her. Family involvement is particularly difficult in schools in poverty areas, where resources are limited and where academic achievement is below average. Yet there are hopeful stories and Family Reading in Central School is one of them.

Each of the seven mothers was interviewed separately by me at Central School in a conference room adjoining the library where Family Reading workshops were usually held. The women knew that I had some connection with the program; they had seen me in the school on previous occasions. To lessen the chance of parents' telling me what they thought I might want to hear, I framed the interview as an occasion for them to give their perspective and to offer suggestions for the program based on their experience. In that way, I said, they would make a contribution to the program.

The interview, guided by a semistructured interview protocol informed by principles of ethnography, elicited mothers' views on what they and their children had learned from the program, their reasons for attending Family Reading workshops, and descriptions of literacy behaviors of both parent and child. Two other categories of questions were intended to evoke "thick" descriptions that would shed additional light on the meaning of the program in the lives of the participants. To elicit information on the place of reading in their family life, the mothers were asked to describe a typical day in their household. To cast light on their current literacy practices, they were asked to describe literacy events from their own childhood; intergenerational research had indicated the power of childhood experience in shaping parental behavior. The mothers were also asked to suggest ways of reaching out to parents who did not attend the program.

All topics were investigated with all respondents, but order of questions and topic duration varied in accordance with its meaningfulness for each individual. Following Spradley (1979), the interview process was recursive, and topics of interest were frequently revisited for additional information. Follow-up probes were also used as needed. Session length averaged 70 minutes. Interviews were audiotaped and transcribed.

The interview sessions were informal and interactive. Consonant with feminist methodology and the belief that the interviewing process is most productive when relationships are nonhierarchical and the interviewer invests personal identity in the relationship the sessions were designed to create connections rather than maintain distance between interviewer and interviewee. For example, during the interview, the mothers occasionally asked me questions about books or reading, to which I responded, and the interview then took on the tone of an ordinary conversational exchange. At intervals I offered brief comments of encouragement or validation. At the end of the session, I asked whether there were additional questions they wanted to ask me and replied to queries about the program or questions about my own family. Displayed on a nearby table was a supply of children's books that I had brought; before leaving, mothers were invited to choose some to take home as a gift. That also gave me an opportunity to observe how they chose books for their children.

The interviews were analyzed inductively; using a grounded theory approach (Strauss & Corbin, 1990) to establish categories and themes. The portrayals of the seven mothers illustrate issues and situations in family literacy. They are not extensive case studies, but tools to think with.

CHAPTER 6

Voices of Mothers

When you are out of school so long . . . you
forget words.

— Ms. Afton

Everyone seems to really come alive during
the Family Reading session. Ms. C. asks
questions and there's a lot of participation. We
all take turns reading a page or a passage
and we talk about the issues and questions
generated by the reading material and we
share experiences. It's a good way to get to
know the other parents and it gives us a lot
of material to talk about when working with
our children. [The teacher] lets us borrow the
books. We take them home, read to our children, bring them back, and practice what we
learned in the session. It's very practical.

— Ms. Smith

I'm not going to lay off. . . . If the child sees
the parent really concerned about the school,
you'd be surprised how the children turn out.

— Ms. Powers

To SHED LIGHT ON the meaning that the Family Reading experience holds
for its participants, the analytic narratives in this chapter and the next will
focus on the mothers' perspectives on the school program and its relationship to their home literacy context. Each interview addressed the mothers'
reasons for attending Family Reading workshops, what they learned, how
their learning is transmitted to their children at home, characteristics of
the home literacy environment, and information about the family literacy
heritage. Issues suggested by the interview material are discussed as well.

INTRODUCING EACH MOTHER

MARGE BURNS

Ms. Burns, age 24, has a 5-year-old son, Tyrell, in kindergarten and a younger son of 17 months. She is a graduate of Central School and of a local high school where she enrolled in a job-training course and received a food preparation certificate. She has worked preparing and packaging meals for the airlines industry at Newark Airport. Her mother, with whom she and the children live, is a retired cafeteria cook. Ms. Burns has attended every Family Reading session during Tyrell's year in kindergarten.

ANN POWERS

Ms. Powers, a physically imposing, voluble woman of 38, has lived in Newark since age 10 and graduated from a Newark high school. She has four children of her own ranging in age from a 20-year-old son to a kindergarten child, Wanda, age 5. Also in the household are a nephew and niece whom she referred to as foster children, who are the children of a sister under treatment for drug addiction. Ms. Powers's mother lives downstairs in the two-family building; Ms. Powers's father has recently reestablished contact with the family after a 35-year absence.

Ms. Powers's interview responses came rolling out in a tide of rambling free association. She was very open in expressing her feelings. However, it was sometimes necessary to interrupt and help her refocus on pertinent questions or to ask for clarifications since she often used pronouns without naming the referent. Ms. Powers has attended three Family Reading sessions and one Family Math session during Wanda's kindergarten year.

ALICIA SMILEY

Ms. Smiley is a small, composed woman of 29 who grew up in Newark, graduated from a local high school, and then attended business school. She has worked as a secretary in the past, but would not consider desk work again, characterizing herself as a "social creature" who likes to be around people. She thinks she might work with children sometime in the future.

Ms. Smiley has two sons, Dwayne, age 5, in kindergarten, and his 16-month-old brother. She held the baby on her lap throughout the interview. She lives alone with the children, but has sisters who live across town. The children's father lives in the area and is active in their upbringing. Ms.

Smiley has attended every Family Reading session during Dwayne's year in kindergarten.

MERCEDES HARRISON SMITH

Ms. Smith, a self-possessed woman of 43, introduced herself using her three names. She has lived in Newark since age 10, and has college and law degrees. She maintains a half-time law practice as a solo practitioner. Ms. Smith and her husband, a minister, have two children, a daughter, Morgana, age 5, in kindergarten, whom tests have shown to be verbally gifted, and a son, age 10, in fifth grade, who reads with a sixth-grade reading group. This was the first year the children were enrolled in Central School. Ms. Smith and her husband have attended every Family Reading session this year.

The Smiths are unique among Family Reading parents in at least two ways. First, few married couples attend the sessions together as they do. Second, and more distinctive, they are highly educated professionals. The Smiths share a mission of helping their community. I was not aware of Ms. Smith's background before interviewing her. The information came as a surprise and naturally sharpened my investigation into her reasons for participating in the program and into what she got out of the school workshops. Ms. Smith seemed fully at ease during the interview; she was articulate and reflective. Because we shared similar goals for the program, during part of the session we discussed ways in which to extend Family Reading into the community.

LINDA GREEN

Ms. Green, who has a child in first grade, has lived in Newark for 17 of her 24 years; she attended Central School and a local high school through Grade 11. In addition to her 6-year-old daughter, Dawnette, she has sons, ages 4½ and 2½, who attend a child care center. The children have different fathers; the sons see their father in the neighborhood, but Dawnette does not have contact with hers. Ms. Green and the children live with her mother and Ms. Green's two sisters, employed by a nursery school and bank, respectively. Ms. Green has 10 siblings, all of whom also attended Central.

Ms. Green has done some cafeteria work in the past, and now volunteers at Central and at her sons' child care center. She came to the interview wearing a large button imprinted with "BOOK LOVER." Throughout she spoke in a rapid, almost hectic tone. She has attended every Family Reading session for 2 years, and is in the school on many other occasions.

SUE AFTON

Ms. Afton, age 29, has one child, her daughter, Keisha, in third grade. A lifelong Newark resident, Ms. Afton graduated from a Newark high school. She works as an aide in an institution for severely retarded adults whom she calls her "children." Ms. Afton is married and lives with her husband, a factory worker, who is also a Newark high school graduate.

Ms. Afton attended almost all the Family Reading sessions when Keisha was in kindergarten. Thereafter she came to two or three sessions a year; her work schedule made it difficult to attend more regularly.

HARRIET BLANK

Ms. Blank, age 42, has 8-year-old twins, one a girl, Sheryl, the other a boy, Brandon, both in third grade. She also has a 24-year-old son. Ms. Blank has lived in Newark and adjacent communities for more than 30 years and has a high school equivalency diploma.

The twins' father lives with the family. He is not in good health and works only occasionally. A Newark high school graduate, he was a corrections officer for 20 years. At the time of the interview, Ms. Blank's older son had been incarcerated for nearly 2 years. She said she believes that he is innocent and thinks he may be released soon. The son is married, with a 2-year-old child. Ms. Blank volunteered the information that she is on welfare. During the interview, she spoke very rapidly, occasionally stuttering in her haste to get the words out.

Ms. Blank has been attending Family Reading for 4 years, since the twins were in kindergarten, and also participates in a Family Math and a parenting program at the school. She said her children "feel proud" that she is involved in their education.

CONTACTS WITH THE SCHOOL

The four women with children in kindergarten are frequently in contact with the school at times other than Family Reading workshops. Ms. Burns, Ms. Powers, Ms. Smiley, and Ms. Smith walk their children to and from school every day and often use the occasion to stop in to talk with the kindergarten teacher and learn what is happening in the classroom. Ms. Blank also maintains contact with the school by walking her third-grade twins to and from school every day. Ms. Smiley and Ms. Smith borrows books from the classroom library between Family Reading sessions; Ms. Powers has made a point of giving Wanda's teacher her phone number and telling her to call should a problem arise. Two of the mothers had long-term familiarity with the school, having attended Central themselves as students; in the case of Ms. Green, so had her numerous siblings. With the exception of Ms. Afton, Family Reading workshops were part of the mothers' continuing contact with the school, rather than their initial or sole contact.

These observations suggest several implications for the process of recruiting parents to attend family literacy programs. The first one is that the presence of parents on school grounds presents an opportunity for outreach by school staff. A welcome by teachers and parents who have participated in family literacy, a few words about the program, inquiries about parents' wishes and needs, and publicity such as eye-catching displays of children's books or photos of participants near the school entrance can all serve to arouse interest on the part of parents who are already in the school. Although this may seem quite obvious, the press of school organization particularly at the busy beginning and end of the day may cause the opportunity to be overlooked. In one school, the presence of mothers congregating in hallways concerned for their children was seen as an interference with routine during the first week of school. Finally, in recognition of the opportunity represented by having parents in the building, a place for them to meet was set up, the mothers were welcomed with coffee, and activities that later burgeoned into a well-attended family reading program were begun.

The second implication is more complicated. While parents of kindergarten and primary-grade children are more likely to be involved with the school than those of older children, additional factors were at work in the case of Central School. Family Reading attracted as a corps of regular mothers who were already connected with the school in some fashion, through informal contacts but also through volunteering, through having attended the school as a student, or through long residence in the neighborhood. Unlike a young woman who came timorously to Family Reading and stiffened when the principal entered the room (he had been her principal not too long ago and the experience had not always been pleasant), the mothers interviewed were comfortable in the familiar school environment. As a group, they seemed to have higher levels of education than most in their community as well. Their profile fits what is called "creaming," the tendency for new or innovative social programs to attract those who are most ready for them, rather than those who are most in need. This has been true of the early years of the federal Even Start program, which has grappled with the issue of whether to serve those with the lowest literacy levels, who are most in need, or those who are ready to learn at higher levels and can attain 12th-grade equivalency relatively quickly.

As in all other schools in the Newark Partnership, the core group

served a function. Not all participants in Family Reading were as well educated or as comfortable in the school as were the seven mothers who had
been selected for interviewing. The core group members helped insure the
continuity of the program, served as program champions to others, and
helped in program dissemination. It is important in the recruitment of participants in family literacy programs—and probably other school projects
as well—that those individuals who come forward, ready to learn, be recognized and appreciated for the role that they play in strengthening program stability and retention.

REASONS FOR ATTENDING FAMILY READING

The seven mothers were asked to talk about their reasons for attending the
Family Reading workshops in order to get a sense of the possible varieties
of reasons and the priorities they may be assigning among those reasons.
Their responses were more elaborated than those in the written surveys,
but fell into similar categories: enjoyment of the participatory nature of the
program; interesting or personally useful content; value for their children;
and individualistic reasons that do not quite fit into those categories.

All of the women appreciated the engaging nature of the workshops.
Specifically, they particularly liked the participatory nature of the program
and the way in which the teacher engaged parents in discussion (Ms.
Burns). Ms. Powers said she enjoyed being with other parents and sharing
stories in the workshops. Ms. Smiley enjoyed "how well" the workshops
went. Ms. Smith also liked the way the workshops provided time for parents to get to know one another. On a more specific level, Ms. Afton and
Ms. Powers particularly mentioned the convenience of borrowing books
from the program; Ms. Afton singled out for appreciation the door prizes
and end-of-year certificates awarded to participants.

The women found the content of the workshops "interesting" (Ms.
Burns). Ms. Afton said she enjoyed the workshop activities and the reading
strategies that were taught. Ms. Powers talked of the many "new" activities
she did not have as a child. When asked what had kept her coming back
to the program for 4 years, Ms. Blank replied,

> It's interesting to me. It teaches you different ways of reading with
> your kids and making fun out of reading material. . . . It makes you
> look at reading in more different ways than just reading the book.
> "The car ran over the dog." It makes you ask questions about it,
> Why did the car run over the dog? I'd suggest it for anybody, not
> just for your child, for yourself.

Ms. Blank especially liked the book discussions, calling each Family Reading session "a new experience not just learning the same thing over and over." A Family Reading enthusiast, Ms. Blank says she will continue coming until the children are in the eighth grade.

Ms. Afton gave two clear reasons for attending Family Reading. The first related to adult learning and the benefits she had obtained from the workshops. Explaining, she said:

> When you are out of school so long you don't read so much . . . your reading level dips . . . you miss things . . . you forget words.

She said that Family Reading helped her see some of the things she had missed or forgotten.

All the women interviewed shared Ms. Afton's second reason for participating in Family Reading, the program's value for children. All liked learning ways in which to interact with their children, enjoyed doing the home activities, and felt their children benefited. Speaking of parent-child relationships Ms. Afton said that children are more motivated to learn if their parents are involved in their schooling and that it was important for parents to teach their children how to read better. She found the information on how to read with children at home and to select age-appropriate books especially helpful. Over the 4-year-period in which Ms. Afton has participated in the program, she has seen how it bolsters Keisha's motivation in school. She reported that the child is always eager for her to attend the workshop sessions.

Ms. Powers said she attends the school programs in reading and math as a way of "encouraging" her child. She likes going to the school because she enjoys the activities and she wants her children to know of her interest.

Ms. Blank also talked about her children's responses and the validation she feels when she shares program experiences with her children; the twins find the reading strategies enjoyable and helpful and they like the books from the program. She was proud too of recognition from teachers because of her participation in the school programs.

When describing the program's value for their children, Ms. Afton, Ms. Powers, and Ms. Blank weave into the conversation their feelings about their children's responses to them as caring adults. That suggests the reciprocity of influence that runs in families engaged in literacy learning and the complexity of family relations in which adults look for recognition from their children even as they are engaged in nurturing them.

The fourth category of reasons for attending Family Reading sessions are individualistic and personal. In the case of Ms. Smiley, to an initial question of what brought her into the program, she responded, "My child, to learn how to read with them, to encourage them, to be helpful." However, later in the interview, she described a strong wish to bring up her children differently from the way in which she was brought up and how Family Reading helps toward that goal. She likes the fact that she "can express (her) opinion" in the workshops and feels that she makes a good contribution to the discussion. Continuing, she said:

> When we go to the meetings and read through the books and look at the pictures and talk about them, I like that. It's telling me how to read, improve my reading skills along with my child. I respect myself.

The opportunity to enhance her own self-esteem seems equally important and integrally connected with her goals for her children.

Ms. Smith and her minister husband are working to develop the Newark community and strengthen the African American family. She said the sessions helped her get to know people on an informal, enjoyable basis, and felt that the workshops themselves helped to promote the goal toward which she was working, that of community solidarity. Describing the community spirit that develops among the groups of parents in the workshop room, she said:

> I know it's okay to read to my kids because, look, there's the other mother reading, and another mother reading to her children, a father reading to his children so this is something we're all doing, so let's keep it up . . . (the workshops) build cohesiveness, then we can go back and read in our individual homes.

For Ms. Smith the community aspect of Family Reading promoted an important social goal.

Like the other parents, Ms. Green reported that she tries to stay involved with school programs for the sake of her children. She expressed pleasure with the Family Reading workshops, praising Ms. Conti, the workshop leader, for "a very good reading program"; she said she was especially "proud" that so many parents had attended. However, Ms. Green's major reason for participating in Family Reading, as will be described more fully later, is the overriding importance in her own life of contact with the school. The Family Reading program had a place as part of her overall relationship with the school.

Ms. Blank also expressed a larger motivation, her strong concern that her children stay interested in education and go on to complete high school. That appears to be the force behind her long participation in Family Read-

ing and in the math and parenting programs at the school. She had emphasized the importance of the diploma to her older son, who graduated from
a local high school, and stresses its importance to her 8-year-old twins
now. Possibly her concern grows out of the experience of her own failure
to graduate through the regular track.

Finally, in concert with the other reasons for her participation, Ms.
Powers indicated the diversionary function for her of the Family Reading
sessions, saying that she liked the feeling the program gave her of "being
kept occupied" and not bothered by the "other problems" of her large and
hectic household.

These mothers' responses indicated a common attentiveness to the education of their children, but also suggested reasons that were personal and
individual to themselves as adults. Thus individuals construct for themselves the meaning of their participation, and the same activity may have
different meanings to different participants. Just as some mothers might
come for the sociability, or the food, or the comfort of a heated building
as reported previously, so the mother interviewed created diverse meanings
for the same Family Reading experience, including personal meanings that
were not initially anticipated by teachers or researcher.

WHAT WAS LEARNED

The mothers functioned as literacy learners in the workshops and as providers of literacy resources to their children, in itself a learning process for
many. They learned substantive knowledge as represented in the workshop
books as well as procedural knowledge, or how to use interactive strategies
with their children. Several mothers picked up books and demonstrated
those strategies during the course of the interview. They had also learned
more about themselves and their children as readers. The mothers' views
about what they had learned, sometimes in response to direct questions in
the interview, sometimes spontaneous or embedded in other remarks, were
colored by expressions of enjoyment of books and of the experiences of
reading to children that the program fostered.

For example, Ms. Afton felt that the interactive strategies made reading fun or gamelike and engaged interest of a type that would lead to better
reading. Ms. Blank said that she enjoys what she learns, stating, "You're
never too old to learn." Ms. Burns reported that she and her son enjoy
reading the workshop books at home. The child is enthusiastic, often urging her to read something to him. Mentioning a particular book, she said
she "could have read that book several times for myself." Ms. Burns also
reported substantive learning from the books and discussion in the work-

shops. "You get to know about other's heritage," she said. Ms. Powers seemed particularly intrigued by a book that described Japanese food customs. Saying that she enjoyed the story, she summarized it during the interview and declared that she wanted to try using chopsticks. She was eager to read it to her daughter Wanda; she wants the kindergartner to "understand the system" because "all she knows is eating with a knife and fork." Ms. Powers envisioned preparing her daughter for going to an Asian restaurant. Ms. Smith said the program had introduced her to "some marvelous new children's books with phenomenal art work" that she enjoys.

Responses such as these demonstrate the importance of the content of the children's books to engagement in the program and to literacy learning. The books were carefully selected to be interesting to adults as well as to children, to represent high-quality text and illustrations, and to deal with nontrivial topics that suggested rich avenues for discussion. Absent those conditions, it is doubtful that strategic learning would have occurred. The teachers' enthusiasm for the workshop books, many of their own selection, must also have been contagious in promoting enthusiasm from participants. A selection of multicultural books was used in the workshops; some related to African American experiences; others did not. The books were intended to serve both as mirrors of one's own experience and as windows into those of others. The African American parents at Central School appeared to enjoy both.

Procedures for using cognitive strategies and employing discussion techniques were major new sources of learning that led in turn to insights about themselves and their children as learners. Ms. Burns reported that she learned "a lot" of procedural strategies such as learning how to "read faster," "asking questions" while reading and relating the pictures to the story. She felt that she had learned how to discuss a story. Before, she would read the book, ask whether her son liked it, and at his "yeah" or "okay" break off the reading without elaboration or discussion. Now, she talks to her son more and asks questions. As a result, she said, she understood why the child wanted repeated readings of a book that was new to him. She said Tyrell had lots of questions and was particularly curious about the book's depiction of the different types of bread in the world. Ms. Burns explained about the various customs and was glad he was learning things outside his everyday experience.

Ms. Smiley's experience was similar. She, too, said she had learned many ideas about reading, including how to exercise imagination and use interactive strategies, such as making predictions by asking her son to look at a book's cover and "say what it is about." Previously, she reported, she would read the pages but wouldn't ask the child anything; she would "just read and let it be":

I would read the pages but wouldn't ask how he would feel. I
wouldn't ask about his imagination. . . . Now, reading he gives me
more insight about what's going on, he asks questions, he might see
colors, like a whole lot of things that's in the book.

Ms. Smiley reported that she now asks Dwayne how he feels about a story
and encourages his questions. The result is that she gets "more insight"
into what the child is thinking. The child has lots of questions and she tries
to figure out the answer or tries to have an answer that he can understand.
Appearing proud of Dwayne's curiosity, Ms. Smiley next picked up a book
about birds from the display table and proceeded to demonstrate an interactive book-reading episode by imitating Dwayne's likely questions about
the book ("Why is that bird flying high? Why is the bird that color?"). "I
try to have an answer," she said.

Ms. Afton, also, indicated that she had learned prediction strategies
and how to generate ideas about a story. That was something new to her,
she said. Saying, "This is how we do," Ms. Afton spontaneously picked up
a children's book from the display table to demonstrate what she had
learned. She asked, "What do you think they are doing in this picture
here?" then read a portion of the text slowly, but correctly, and asked,
"What do you think *kente* is? . . . You read, then tell some ideas you have,"
she explained. Both she and Ms. Smiley appeared eager to demonstrate
how they interacted with their children.

When reading with her 8-year-old daughter, Ms. Afton enjoys applying the strategies learned in the workshops. She likes drawing out the
child's ideas and does not mind if they differ from her own. Evoking the
spirit of the workshops, she said, "Everybody has different ideas. That's
what it's all about." She added that it was "fun" to discuss ideas with
Keisha because she had "good ideas" and was "pretty smart." In addition,
Ms. Afton felt that her own vocabulary knowledge had improved as a
result of Family Reading.

Ms. Blank also enjoys the give and take of ideas with her 8-year-old
son and daughter. She has adopted the practice of discussion, "allowing
everybody to give their own opinion," and of predicting what is going to
happen in the story. She said that was more interesting than "just reading."
She talks to her children about the Family Reading workshops and the
children like that. One consequence of her participation is that both she
and the children are reading more as well as using the interactive reading
strategies. It seems likely that Family Reading has helped Ms. Blank establish an age-appropriate reading relationship with the twins characterized
by discussion and reciprocal questioning about books.

Ms. Blank went on to point out that she would probably read even without the program, but not the way she does now, with a high degree of involvement. She said she had "learned a lot" from Family Reading, to "look at a book differently," to "really go into the book, saying this could happen" or "what if this had been different" or "what if they had done this." In short, she indicated she had learned to read thoughtfully and to explore alternatives.

Ms. Smith, an attorney, is a skilled reader herself. What had she learned from the workshops? First, referring to a major reason for her participation, she said she had gained an understanding of the other parents by joining with them in the workshops. She had learned what things they are comfortable talking about and now felt more comfortable communicating with them. She said she knew relationships could be difficult because of "stereotypes in the back of (her) mind" about the other less advantaged parents. Compounding the difference in education and occupation, Ms. Smith pointed out that she is almost a generation older than many Family Reading participants.

Significantly for literacy development, Ms. Smith also reported that she had learned the value of asking questions when reading to children. Although she was accustomed to asking herself questions during her own reading, as is characteristic of good readers, the process was an automatic one (Afflebach & Johnson, 1986) and needed to be brought to a level of conscious awareness in order to be applied when reading with children. The Family Reading workshops made the strategy explicit and helped her realize its appropriateness for children. After having learned techniques for teaching cognitive strategies, Ms. Smith said, "Reading becomes more than just reading . . . it becomes an interactive session with you and the child." In common with the other mothers, she also acquired cultural knowledge from the workshop books.

Ms. Smith's new use of interactive techniques also influenced her selection of books for her daughter. Realizing that discussing a book will make more demanding texts accessible, she now selects longer books, knowing that she can hold her daughter's attention through initiating discussion and raising questions about the story. She said she was pleased at exploring books she would not have thought age appropriate. Ms. Smith said that was a difference from the other reading programs for children in which she had participated.

Ms. Smith's case is one in which the perspectives of parent and educator had initially diverged, with the parent coming to understand the significance of the educators' instruction. Despite her middle-class status and advanced degree, Ms. Smith demonstrated that she had something to learn from educators. This is an important understanding for educators and an indication that they have professional knowledge to share with all parents, regardless of socioeconomic background. Although directed mainly to families in poverty, programs such as Family Reading can be meaningful to more advantaged families as well. Indeed, many teachers report that middle-class and affluent families are not familiar with the variety of good children's books available and often have not established a habit of regular reading with their children. Family Reading has spread to these other types of communities in various parts of the country. Teachers in graduate courses at my university have adapted elements of the program in their suburban schools and find parents eager for knowledge about books and how and when to read to their children.

The two mothers not yet discussed, Ms. Green and Ms. Powers, are exceptions to the focus on learning reading strategies. Ms. Green was not specific about strategies that she might have learned in the workshops, saying merely that she had learned "actually a lot of things" that she wanted to do with her children and pointing out that she reads to all three even though her first grader also reads to herself. However, she volunteered substantive knowledge about a book recently presented in the workshop, paraphrasing the story and offering several generalizations about the plot and characters.

Ms. Powers was not articulate about the reading strategies either. She referred to them as "tips" and "exercises" for literal comprehension. Although she reported learning that discussing a book with her child would provide an idea of the child's thinking, she offered no further elaboration or example of actual practice. During the interview, however, she spontaneously demonstrated one program strategy, relating reading to personal experience. When choosing a gift book to take home at the conclusion of the interview, she was excited to spot one called *Josephine's Imagination*, with a picture on the cover of a barefoot Black girl in a rural setting:

> That's just like me . . . I let my imagination go. I tell my children I walked two miles to school, sometimes I had shoes on, sometimes not.

Ms. Powers also said that the program gave her "more insight" into reading and that she now knew that "sometimes you have to read the entire book to understand the main idea." Although she did not mention any reading strategies or interactive discussion with her daughter, Ms. Powers said the program was prompting her to get back into reading for herself after family pressures had caused her to slacken off.

In her interview, Ms. Powers described her practice of telling stories at home, particularly ones with family or self-referential themes. Because of her greater familiarity and comfort with storytelling, instruction in the cognitive strategies as applied to storytelling, rather than text reading, might have been a way in which to help Ms. Powers think more analytically. Put another way, following the principle of relating new information, in this case, procedural knowledge, to something familiar, the genre of storytelling, might have enabled her to make a better transition to book reading involving the use and awareness of strategies. Again, it is clear that she liked the books and was aware of some ways of constructing meaning from print, as seen by her comment about sometimes having to read extended text in order to understand the main idea.

Unlike compulsory education for children, most family literacy programs are voluntary. Although adults may participate because they foresee economic benefits from getting a GED or from becoming an American citizen now that the safety net for noncitizens is being eliminated, and literacy is necessary to meet these goals, continued commitment usually requires strong motivation given the stresses in their daily lives and their possible unfamiliarity with the work of literacy learning. In family literacy programs, the participants' strong desire to help their children coupled with the children's enthusiasm and encouragement of their parents' attendance often provides such motivation. This synergistic relationship is one of the strengths of family literacy. It has also been pointed out that "parents are more likely to support children's learning when they see themselves as effective learners" (Nickse et al., 1988). Accordingly, the programmatic content for adults is important in maintaining commitment and fulfilling the essential goal of family literacy programs.

The mothers' reasons for participating in Family Reading and the learning gained from that participation are mutually reinforcing situations. There is a great deal of overlap between the two descriptions. That is only natural, since participation was voluntary and no one could be expected to attend on a regular basis unless they found something of value in the program. The topics were distinguished in order to clarify conditions and to explore some of the issues suggested by the responses. As before, the responses indicated that the mothers were functioning both as literacy learners and as literacy resources to their children. With the exceptions noted, their literacy behaviors with their children now included strategy use and discussion, an expansion of previous practice. In addition, although family closeness was not described as a value as explicitly as in the survey responses, the enjoyable reading relationship with children was much prized.

CHAPTER 7

Literacy Resources in the Home Environment

School is like a relative to me.
—Ms. Green

Sometimes we have a little family thing . . .
We sit at the table and read together.
—Ms. Afton

If my parents had a choice, if they knew what
was going on and going 'round then they
would have read to me.
—Ms. Smiley

WHAT WAS THE HOME CONTEXT of the reading interactions with children on the part of Family Reading participants? What place did reading have in the household, what other literacy activities and resources were available, and how did the family literacy heritage of the mothers influence their child-rearing practices? Although children are not a focus of this chapter, the portrayals of home environments provide additional glimpses of their feelings and reactions.

The seven different home environments described here round out the picture of family reading interactions attributable to what was learned in the Family Reading workshops. The headings represent major themes derived from the interviews with the mothers.

ENLARGING THE LITERACY EXPERIENCE OF THE HOME

When Marge Burns was asked for further descriptions of reading practices at home, she said that she reads to Tyrell and his brother at night when "it is quiet." She wants the children to go to sleep with a good feeling about themselves. Tyrell expresses his eagerness by saying, "You going to read to me tomorrow night too?" Ms. Burns enjoys the reading sessions and tries to read every night. She said:

> It makes me feel good to read to him . . . it's like communicating love. . . . We get to talk and everything.

Occasionally, Tyrell's grandmother will read to him during the day if he approaches her with a book. His 17-month-old brother likes singing and nursery rhymes and listening to a story for 5 or 10 minutes at bedtime, which Ms. Burns says is "good for now."

Ms. Burns also helps with homework, especially spelling, which the teacher had advised was a weak subject for Tyrell. On days when he has a new spelling word, Tyrell will spell it and his mother will help him. Sometimes, Ms. Burns will "make up" homework for him based on his classwork. Ms. Burns does not do much reading for herself beyond a newspaper "some mornings" or maybe a magazine or *TV Guide*.

Television is an important part of the household routine. The children watch *Barney* or other children's shows before school. Tyrell watches after school as well, although he first must brief his mother on school events or any test coming up. Ms. Burns says that *Sesame Street* is a favorite show and she feels the children have learned from it. For example, the 17-month-old has learned number sequences; if she says "1," he'll say "2"; when she says "3," he'll say "4"; and so on to 10.

Ms. Burns spontaneously mentioned that she has been purchasing books through the mail for 5-year-old Tyrell almost from birth. Coupons come in the mail from a book service offering books on a trial basis. She assumes that the company got her name and address from the hospital where Tyrell was born. The service offers age-appropriate books, mainly Dr. Seuss and *Sesame Street* at this stage. A free bookshelf and alphabet cards have also been obtained.

Ms. Burns also reported important experiences beyond the home, involving use of community resources. From age 2 on, Tyrell had attended a private preschool run by the Urban League. According to Ms. Burns, the preschool's advanced curriculum accounts for the child's familiarity with colors and signs and his success in kindergarten now. Next year, she plans to enroll him in the local Boys Club, where he can swim and do homework after school. Ms. Burns also arranges trips to Disneyworld and summer visits to out-of-state relatives. She presents Tyrell as a curious and energetic child who loves to travel, even if it's just to the mall.

When asked about reading to Tyrell, Ms. Burns spontaneously recalled that her mother read to her when she was growing up. Although the occasions were infrequent, because of the mother's work, they were apparently specially prized. Her mother read to her, Ms. Burns reported, whenever she was home. In addition, an aunt read to her often. Ms. Burns recalled that many of the books she purchases for Tyrell—*The Cat in the Hat, Bears on Wheels*, pop-up books—are the same as those she heard when she was a child. Asked about family stories, Ms. Burns remembered stories told at family reunions and her eagerness to hear them.

Overall, Family Reading enlarged the literacy environment of a home in which the mother was concerned to provide literacy opportunities as well as experiences in the larger world that support learning. The Family Reading workshops themselves were valued for their participatory nature. Ms. Burns had learned interactive discussion techniques and uses them when reading to her child. No carryover into her own reading was reported; rather the children's books represent a continuation of her own childhood experiences.

A HECTIC HOUSEHOLD WITH TIME FOR STORYTELLING

Storytelling is the most elaborated literacy activity in Ann Powers's home. At bedtime, Ms. Powers tells Wanda stories about her childhood. She does not reveal that the story is about herself, but leaves the little girl curious to learn more. "Who is this girl?" she reports Wanda will ask. "She grew up to be a nice young lady," the mother replies. Someday, Ms. Powers will tell her who it is. Right now, she seems to be enjoying the child's fascination with her tales. Ms. Powers used to tell stories to her older daughter (now 18) who sometimes passes them on to Wanda in turn.

Ms. Powers's storytelling is a continuation of a family tradition. She reported that her mother did not read, but told her many stories about sharecropper life in the South. She particularly liked stories about the farm animals, about what her mother's life was like in the time before electricity, and about her grandparents, who were also sharecroppers and storytellers. She believes that her father also told stories. Ms. Powers grew up with seven siblings and, as the oldest girl, took care of the younger ones. She said she learned the stories she was told and when she had children of her own she knew them to tell.

To a query about reading in the household, Ms. Powers said that she reads magazines and also watches the news on television. She reports that she has "always been a reader" but that she slackened off after she took on the care of her niece (age 3) and nephew (age 11) prior to Wanda's kindergarten year. The increased responsibility also meant less reading to

Wanda. Ms. Powers had been accustomed to reading to her at bedtime "whatever books (she) could get"; *Goldilocks* and *The Little Engine That Could* were mentioned. She reads books borrowed from Family Reading and, saying she is now into books as well as storytelling, hopes that the program will stimulate her adult reading as well. Wanda's older sister occasionally reads to her, and Wanda herself "reads" and plays "make-believe" with her younger cousin. The children in the family also help one another with homework.

When asked about a typical day in her large household, Ms. Powers laughed and said, "It can be hectic, *very* hectic." She described her day largely in terms of whether or not she had "problems" with one or another of the children, but also mentioned efficiency measures she uses to ease the household routine. She says the children are not rowdy, but often help with chores and that the older ones assist the younger ones with homework.

Describing a major problem with her nephew who "didn't listen" to his classroom teacher and refused to do homework, Ms. Powers said she intervened at the school on his behalf and, on the principal's advice, spent time sitting in his classroom to show him that she was involved and concerned. With all the children a continuing issue was their reluctance to get organized in the morning.

The school's Family Math program is also important to Ms. Powers. Math today, she emphasized, was *hard*; she would like to help her high school daughter with algebra and trigonometry, but simply cannot. She appreciates the math "tips" she has learned and hopes they will be useful in helping Wanda and her 11-year-old nephew.

Reporting an important literacy experience outside the home, Ms. Powers described attending a program for welfare recipients at a community college in which she learned the reading skills of finding the main idea and recognizing topic sentences. The program included preschool for Wanda. Crediting the preschool for Wanda's easy transition and good performance in kindergarten (she entered "knowing how to count to 10 and spell her name") Ms. Powers says she will see that her niece is enrolled in the future.

Ms. Powers wants her children to have more opportunities than she had. Although she characterized her childhood as "pretty nice," her early life in the South had its difficulties. She speaks of having to walk two miles to school, to impress upon her children the privileges they have today, she said. She was especially pleased that her elder daughter wants to go to college and is trying for a scholarship. One of her worries, however, was the contrast between her "safe" childhood and the violence today.

In the interview, all information concerning reading resulted from my questions; none was volunteered or incorporated into Ms. Powers's account of a typical day, although, when prompted, Ms. Powers recounted details of literacy activities in the home. For Ms. Powers it appears that reading and homework activities are secondary to household management and concerns about child behavior. This makes sense of course, for she feels overburdened at home with the six children. Under the circumstances, it is commendable that Ms. Powers attends so many school meetings and wishes to learn from them. She views the school programs in reading and math as resources that enable her to help her children achieve. It is hard to know what more can realistically be expected of individuals in Ms. Powers's situation. Possibly programs that reach out to older siblings in the family or provide parent mentors might ease some of the burden.

Family Reading sessions are supportive for Ms. Powers, however, since she regards them as a diversion from other worrisome concerns. In addition, they have stimulated her to resume reading. She also reported trying to recruit other parents into the Family Reading program.

Although it appears that Ms. Powers has learned some reading strategies in the Family Reading workshops, transfer of that learning to reading experiences with her daughter is yet to be made. Recency of her own incorporation of the reading strategies, insufficient awareness of their importance, or a personal expressive style that precludes the more reflective pace of strategy use are possible explanations for the apparent lack of transfer to the home setting. As suggested earlier, it may be that a storytelling, rather than a text-reading instructional approach to the strategies might have fostered more progress incorporating the strategies. On the other hand, the content of the books aroused Ms. Powers's interest and she volunteered ways in which she could extend that information to her daughter. Most promising, Ms. Powers projects a great sense of responsibility toward working with her children. She said:

> I am not going to lay off. You have to be a concerned parent. If the child sees the parent really concerned about the school, you be surprised how the children turn out.

DETERMINED TO BE DIFFERENT

Alicia Smiley has been in the habit of reading to her son Dwayne for several years. Last year she read for 15 minutes every morning. It was a time to get to "know one another better and have mutual respect." She feels that the reading sessions helped Dwayne when he was in preschool.

In addition to her reading that involves interactive questioning, Ms. Smiley reads to both children at bedtime "to get them settled" and help them feel comfortable about going to sleep. She likes to read them "good books, not horror stories that could give them bad dreams." Ms. Smiley volunteered the information that she buys books for Dwayne such as *The Cat in the Hat*, through a mail order firm, perhaps the same one used by Ms. Burns. Dwayne recognized words in the Dr. Seuss book that appear in his school workbook, she said.

Television is a major interest for Dwayne. "It's like that TV is calling his name." He watches MTV after school and is reluctant to do any homework. Ms. Smiley lets him watch, then insists he do homework. On weekends, Ms. Smiley lets 5-year-old Dwayne choose his activities. "I give him a decision, what he wants to do, play or read a book for instance; it's his decision." Most of the time Dwayne decides to play.

Responding to a query, Ms. Smiley said the program had definitely stimulated her to read for herself as well. She borrows pamphlet material about parenting and books about reading comprehension and nursery rhymes available in the school.

Ms. Smiley had long seen herself as an agent in her son's education. When Dwayne was 2 years old, Ms. Smiley reported, she undertook to create what she called "a school in the home." The idea was sparked by a little bubble gum machine she had bought. Whenever the child wanted a piece of gum, she would ask him to name its color. From this serendipitous beginning, she began to teach shapes and letters and to read to him. Ms. Smiley felt her teaching sessions at home helped Dwayne when he was in preschool.

Ms. Smiley described her own upbringing as very different from the way in which she is raising her family now. She reported that her wish to make things better for her children is the reason she is so interested in Family Reading and another school program that deals with parenting. Her mother died when she was 5, leaving her father with six children. She says she could not talk to her parents when she was little and that in the family home children were always told what to do. To the query of whether she was read to or heard stories as a child, she answered no, but said had her parents known of its importance they would have read to her. "If my parents had a choice, if they knew what was going on and going 'round then they would have read to me," she said.

Her statement is important in its faith in the goodwill of her parents had they only known what to do. Although there are some exceptions, such as adults trapped in the closed world of drug addiction or violence, experience shows that parents, however poor or lacking in formal education, are dedicated to the welfare of their children. Developing awareness of the importance of reading to children is a prime aim of family literacy programs, as is its corollary: making sure that parents have the operational skills to implement that awareness, and an understanding of what reading to children entails, the ways in which it can be done, and the likely consequences. This increased awareness is what Family Reading participants are showing.

Ms. Smiley believes that she can change the pattern of behavior she experienced as a child. When Dwayne was born, she knew did not want to follow her parents' example and sought alternatives. Hoping the child would learn from her behavior, she started business school classes, read to him, and was "more of a mom than a friend." She feels she can do many things differently for her children, including reading at home and allowing her son to make some decisions. She said she wants to have a relationship with her children and be part of their lives:

> I know I can stop the pattern. You know, talk to him, have a relationship, talk about anything. We have choices now. I was the first to break this pattern. I wanted to, and I tell my sisters you don't have to be like that.

Somewhat paradoxically, Ms. Smiley said that because behaviors are learned from parents and she recognizes that she and her siblings learned from her father, she knows that she can change and have a different effect on her children. Ms. Smiley said she was the first to break the family pattern; she encourages her sisters to do likewise. They, being somewhat skeptical, call her the "preacher" in the family.

The participatory aspects of Family Reading workshops, particularly the encouragement to express her own opinion, are important to Ms. Smiley. She values autonomy for her son as well, as exemplified in giving him a choice of activities on weekends. Ms. Smiley had created a reading environment in her home prior to Family Reading, but added interactive discussion as a result of her participation. Ms. Smiley's break with family history and determination to create a different type of family relationship lends urgency to her involvement with school programs. Family Reading serves to support and validate her goal.

LITERACY IN A LARGER CONTEXT

The interview with Mercedes Smith was more extensive than those with the other mothers. An articulate person, she was eager to discuss many aspects of literacy and schooling. Although her thoughtful mode of expression may reflect her educational status and contrast with those of the others, the activities and feelings described have many similarities. The resources available in the Smith home with two highly educated parents are likely to be more plentiful, however.

Ms. Smith regards reading as one part of her children's lives, a taken-for-granted rather than a special or noteworthy event. Reading is "one of the healthy activities" that her children can choose to do. She said she does not dictate when the children must read, but rather, suggests that they might like to read as one of their choices. Sometimes, she said with a smile, her son will choose to play basketball.

Ms. Smith presented a picture of literacy as a valued activity that is incorporated into many aspects of the Smith household. Like the Aftons, the Smith parents read the Bible at home together with their children. Other home activities appear to reinforce and build on school learning. For example, when Morgana delighted her mother by learning to read and spell a number of words through using a kindergarten computer, Ms. Smith took her to the library and they found four small books that the child could read by herself. Library visits are frequent.

Ms. Smith sometimes reads to both her daughter and 10-year-old son at the same time. Because the children may have different reactions to the story, she puts the interactive techniques into the service of promoting good sibling relationships. "It's a good time to teach them to respect the other child's point of view," she said.

Noting differences between the children, Ms. Smith said her daughter tends to have more "abstract or creative reactions" to books, whereas her son "is much more practical in his responses." She attributed this to gender differences and the fact that the boy has attended "too many different schools" and so tries to come up with answers that are "acceptable or reasonable." Finding a book they both enjoy is "a challenge, but worth it" Ms. Smith said. Her son, who likes adventure, science, and books of facts or statistics, is very particular about likes and dislikes, but her daughter's taste in books is broader.

Ms. Smith usually reads to the children at bedtime, but lately has been trying to read to them in the middle of afternoon. She said that she tells the children to shut off the TV and get a book.

Ms. Smith went on to say that her daughter's experience with interactive strategies has made the child more comfortable in extending her reading abilities. Morgana does not feel bad when encountering words she does not know and is not afraid to take a guess. She is now likely to initiate questions during book-reading sessions, whereas previously her mother asked all the questions. Mr. Smith also reads to his daughter, but the child apparently prefers her mother's more dramatic delivery.

Ms. Smith said that the program stimulated her to read more for herself and, although Bible reading was a previously established practice, caused her to regard reading as a family, and not just an individual, activity. In addition, Ms. Smith serves as a writing model. She attends a writing program at a local university and has completed several short pieces, including an African American version of *Goldilocks* called *Ebony Locks*, which she has shared with her children. Ms. Smith agreed to read the story to parents at the next Family Reading session.

Although Ms. Smith gives her children choices, she has strong views on several subjects. On the subject of television, Ms. Smith compared it unfavorably to reading. She was concerned with the issue of parental control over what children experience:

> I know what the book is about, but I don't know what's coming on the TV . . . what language is going to come out . . . or what will be on the commercial.

Ms. Smith values the knowledge of human relationships that reading can provide, saying that you can "really get to know some people there on the page" and "in this day of anonymity, nobody knows anybody else, nobody cares." She called reading a basis for society, and a source of information and enjoyment as well as community.

Ms. Smith spoke of the need to nurture the dormant creative potential in the Black community. She was less certain about the role of the school, however. She said that schools may emphasize thinking skills but not provide enough factual information for children to build on. She recognized that while wide reading helps children learn to write and speak "standard English," of which she approved, many children do not read a great deal and perhaps should be taught standard usage directly through diagramming sentences, as she had been.

In the past, Ms. Smith has served as a volunteer, talking to community groups about the value of reading aloud to children. She remarked that for many parents the concept of reading to children was a "totally novel idea." As for her own case, she cited three reasons why it appeared natural to her: cultural information as a result of her educational level; advice in child-rearing books such as Dr. Spock's that she read when awaiting her first child; and "family heritage," the example and precept of her mother, who read to her and encouraged her to do so with her own children. Ms. Smith's mother apparently still fosters literacy; she has encouraged Ms. Smith to submit her *Ebony Locks* story for publication.

Sharing her husband's ministry of working for community betterment, Ms. Smith saw Family Reading as a way of bonding with community residents despite age and socioeconomic-status differences. The experiences in Family Reading workshops provided a common bond and helped her "feel a part of the others." She felt that she could now communicate with other parents about local problems and they with her.

Ms. Smith portrayed her various roles and activities as part of an integrated whole. She said she did not separate out her role as a parent from her community work or her involvement in Family Reading from her religious life. Although a strong supporter of Family Reading in Central School, she was uncertain about the effectiveness of some modern pedagogy.

Ms. Smith exemplifies the educated, fluent reader for whom the processes of comprehension are so automatic that they are normally inaccessible to conscious awareness (Afflebach & Johnson, 1986; Garner, 1987). Cognitive strategies were so integrated and automatic in Ms. Smith's reading, that they had dropped below the level of awareness until they were explicitly demonstrated in Family Reading workshops. As a result, she began using questioning strategies when reading with her daughter. Ms. Smith's experience indicated the utility of family literacy program for highly educated individuals as well as for those who are less advantaged.

THE SCHOOL AS HAVEN

In her interview, Linda Green focused on the overall literacy environment of her home and her own relationship to the school. She spoke of few specific incidents of Family Reading influences on the home. However, she reported that she reads several books to all three of her children in the late afternoon. She said that they are interested and quiet when she does so, and that the first grader, Dawnette, will read by herself as well. Reading and homework precede watching television. Ms. Green borrows books from the school and also subscribes to the same books-by-mail service as the other mothers.

Ms. Green appeared sensitive to her children's developmental level. For example, she tried to teach her older boy to write his name when he was 3, but quickly saw that he was not ready. She tried again a year later and was happy when he could do it. Ms. Green said she praises her children's achievements; when they bring papers home from school or preschool she posts them on the wall. Recently one of the boys was drawing pictures; "I felt good," she said.

About twice a month, Ms. Green takes the children to the public library to borrow books and tapes and participate in library programs. Learning from a school counselor about children's programs at a museum, Ms. Green said she plans to take them there too. She felt her children were sometimes bored because they were "very bright."

Ms. Green has recently begun reading for her own personal purposes, mentioning a book of meditations in particular:

One book I have that will help me is called *Black Pearls*; the author is Colvin, I think. I was going to bring it. . . . Passages in there say to take 5 minutes out of your time today to think about accomplishing your goals. It's really good and the meditations that go by dates, but I just read them [through].

Ms. Green does not remember reading or being read to when she was a child. She could not explain the emphasis on literacy in her own household but merely said that she was "definitely different" from her sisters and that she kept to herself most of the time. She presented herself as an isolated individual even though there are three other adults in the household.

Quite beyond the participation in Family Reading, Newark schools play a supportive role in Ms. Green's life. She maintains contact with her high school teachers, especially her typing teacher, with whom she has had an 8-year connection. At Central School, she talks to the social workers, principal and teachers. She said,

The school is so willing to help me and I see this. School is like a relative to me. . . . When I see someone trying to help me I go for it.

Ms. Green is a presence at Central School. She volunteers in Dawnette's classroom, in the library, and on the playground. She talks to many of the teachers, who encourage her and "pick [her] up." Ms. Green reported that she is "depressed a lot." She meets with the school counselor and seeks help from Dawnette's present and former teachers.

Ms. Green reported pleasure at her interaction with children in the school. She tells them stories and feels that they look up to her and become attached to her. She said some of the staff who observe her with children comment on her teaching skill. She reported a wish to become a teacher herself.

When I asked the reason for all the volunteering (she also assists at her sons' child care center), Ms. Green replied,

I just love getting up in the morning when the kids get up. . . . What else would I be doing, wasting time, when I could be going to the school.

School seems to be a place where she is accepted, exercises her abilities, and receives both gratification and help.

Ms. Green also stated that on the advice of the school counselor she planned to read a lot of educational texts, because she wanted to teach. She realized the need for further education to become a teacher, but her plans were vague. At one time, she had started in a special program at a community college, but lasted only a few days because of disruption to the children's schedule. At the end of the interview, after mentioning teaching as a possible goal, Ms. Green said she wanted to "have it all" and would love to act and be a comedian. Was that remark an example of her lack of focus? Was it stimulated by her experience working with children and a recognition of the performance aspects of teaching? Would she be able to use her exuberance in productive ways whether in the service of a teaching career or otherwise? Those are unanswered questions that the interview with Ms. Green evoked.

After the interview, I sought comments from the Family Reading facilitator, who had known her for 2 years. According to this teacher, Ms. Green has been "in and out" of GED testing at the community college. The teacher believes that "something is shooting her down." She said Ms. Green has mood swings and complains that her siblings do not want her to advance herself.

In summary, Ms. Green seems to be a bright individual who relies on the school as a source of self-esteem and support. Despite encouragement from teachers, she has not yet been able to proceed with her own education. However, she is committed to the Family Reading program and tries to get other parents to attend. She is also energetic in fostering literacy in her home and uses reading for her own personal development.

A FOCUS ON MOTIVATION

The Afton family is unique in the sample, being composed of a married couple and only one child. The interview data suggest a cohesive family that does things together with parental responsibility and influence on motivation a strong theme. Although by her own admission Sue Afton is not an able reader, she has been energetic in providing books for her child, inventing ways to teach her, and incorporating interactive strategies from the program into home learning. Particularly notable is her openness to discussion with the child.

As described, the Afton household seemed calm and organized. Ms. Afton said that Keisha kisses her and tells her she loves her every morning. When returning from school, Keisha does homework first, then watches TV; reading happens every night after supper. Ms. Afton portrayed a cohesive family life with mother, father, and child engaging in many joint activities, including reading. She said:

> Sometimes we have a little family thing and we all sit at the table and read together. We each read separately and we each read aloud to one another. We mainly do things as a family . . . go to the park or library together. That's what makes the children want to learn, when they see parents willing to participate in some of the things they like.

As in the Smith household, the family reads the Bible together, and will sometimes read the newspaper or watch and discuss the news on television.

Ms. Afton said that she read to and with Keisha every night after dinner. She described a reciprocal reading arrangement appropriate to her daughter's development. First, she lets Keisha read some pages, then she reads some. Then Keisha might pick out another book she likes and read to her mother.

In earlier years, Ms. Afton reported that she might ask her daughter to recall story events or identify a character, but, when she started attending Family Reading workshops, she incorporated strategies from the program into a "system" she had developed earlier.

What Ms. Afton called her system was a deliberate, organized plan that included interesting Keisha in reading at an early age through frequent library visits. She said she started Keisha off with books that had familiar pictures or dealt with familiar situations, then found books with easy words, and then books with bigger words as she got older. She would read to Keisha, show her the words, and have the child repeat them. In that way, she said, Keisha learned words for size, shape, time, and color.

Ms. Afton reported that Keisha had "lots of books," perhaps 20 or 25, including books about Black history, Dr. Seuss books, children's books about God, and Bible stories. Keisha also has tapes of books, receives books as presents, and borrows books from the library and school. Ms. Afton subscribes to the books-by-mail service for her. She added that Keisha was now on the honor roll at school.

Ms. Afton appeared to enjoy talking about the children's books. She laughed, remembering a *Curious George* story that Keisha brought home from kindergarten. She and Keisha made bathtub toys modeled after those in the book.

Expressing the need for children to have a good education and parents' responsibility to help them get it, Ms. Afton said that teachers could not do the entire job themselves. More immediately, she felt reading was valuable because it kept children off the streets, which are "bad" now.

Most of Ms. Afton's information about home literacy was volunteered, but she was not expansive about her own adult reading. She said she read a lot; a specific title she recalled was *Of Mice and Men.*

When asked about her own childhood, Ms. Afton remembered her mother reading to her and telling stories. Among the books were Dr. Seuss and other books that "are the same that kids have today." Her mother also provided records to go with the books, and they would play them over and over. Ms. Afton said she did the same thing with Keisha, for "that's how children learn by listening over and over." The childhood family storytelling tradition continues when Ms. Afton, her sisters, and mother get together.

At the conclusion of the interview, when I was complying with Ms. Afton's request to relate something of my own history, a remark about poetry prompted her to add the information that her mother writes poems for family occasions. She writes birthday poems for Ms. Afton instead of buying a card, and when a son died the mother wrote poetry about him. Ms. Afton said she would ask her mother to read some of her poems at a Family Reading workshop.

ENTHUSIASM AND A SECOND CHANCE

Harriet Blank reported home-reading experiences spontaneously and with a great deal of zest. She said her children "count on her" to support their reading. That was a "big thing" for her. She and the children like to share books. Ms. Blank said she will say,

> "Oh, I've read this book myself," and the children say, "Mom, do you remember I found this. . . . " Then we discuss the book. It helps them.

At this stage, she said Sheryl was more interested in reading than was her brother. Sometimes Ms. Blank reads with her in the morning before school. Describing their interaction, Ms. Blank said,

> Sheryl will read a page and exclaim "Ain't that something!" I'll say "Can you imagine!" We discuss each page, discuss anything that comes to mind.

Then they start asking each other questions about the story.

The twins occasionally read to one another and argue about the story.

Their mother approved their expression of opinion. In addition, Sheryl reads aloud to younger relatives. Sometimes she will choose to read whereas her brother will watch television. Ms. Blank reported that Sheryl will read "anything," whereas Brandon prefers books about sports and cars. From the selection of gift books for the interview, she chose a story about imagination as a topic that both children would like.

The twins read with their father as well as their mother and will ask him questions about what he is reading. Having attended an occasional Family Reading workshop himself and hearing about others from Ms. Blank, the father also is knowledgeable about interactive reading strategies.

The household has a large dictionary; when the children don't know the meaning of a word, Ms. Blank says, "Look it up! That's what the dictionary is for." She urges similar independence on them when they come across a word they cannot pronounce, refusing to read it for them and telling them to sound it out for themselves.

There is no set time for reading in the Blank family. Rather, reading occurs on the spur of the moment when the children want it or when a family members has something interesting to share. Most reading tends to occur on Sunday when the family reads the newspaper.

Ms. Blank reported that if she sees a book in the store, she buys it and brings it home. "It's fun to them," she says. She also mentioned Walt Disney books that come through a mail subscription. Ms. Blank especially encouraged reading in the summers. At the close of school, she said she would borrow math and science textbooks for them to study in preparation for the next school year. She is proud that the children's school grades have improved.

Both parents began buying books for the twins when they were in a Head Start preschool at age 3. The books were skill oriented—identifying the alphabet, writing the letters, identifying colors. Ms. Blank remembered teaching the twins and being surprised when Brandon recognized letters and words in a newspaper she was reading. In addition to books, the twins have Scrabble Jr., which they play every day, and a game called Spello that helps with vocabulary.

Ms. Blank said she is reading more now than she ever did, although her own reading appears to be mainly children's books and the newspaper. She reads the children's books as a way of getting the children interested. Her own enthusiasm for learning shows through in the book discussions with her children and also in her attendance at school programs.

Recently, Ms. Blank has begun advocating for the teaching of more Black history in the school, an activism prompted by a book on famous African Americans that the children's father brought home for them. Ms. Blank discovered that her sports-minded son had never heard of Jackie

Robinson. That so shocked her and the book so interested her that she brought the book to the attention of the PTA and the children's teachers.

Asked about her childhood literacy experiences, Ms. Blank offered a brief recollection of reading books as a child and hearing some stories from her sisters. She did not remember being read to by a parent; her mother had to raise the family of six children alone and worked two jobs. Ms. Blank then quickly turned to a description of her relationship with her older son, which appeared to be a more significant influence on her child rearing now. Barely 18 when he was born, Ms. Blank described difficult times. Within 8 days of the birth, the boy's father died. The child was raised mainly by his grandmother; Ms. Blank did not spend much time with him, although she successfully impressed upon him the necessity for a high school diploma. Ms. Blank said that she regretted her lack of care and had expressed this to her son (now 24). When the twins were born, she resolved to "make it [her] business to be a better parent; I didn't do it then, but I'm going to do it now," she said. Ms. Blank also takes pleasure in buying books and reading to her little grandchild.

Ms. Blank's participation in school programs and her energy in fostering literacy in her home appear to represent a second chance, a way to compensate for her relative inattentiveness to her first child as well as to express her convictions about parental responsibility now. She appears to have adopted Family Reading's interactive reading and discussion strategies and to have incorporated them into an enjoyable reading relationship with her children. In this, she is supported by the children's father and by interaction between the siblings.

This core group of women who were interviewed helped ensure the success of Family Reading. We may ask whether they were typical of others who attended Family Reading. They were better educated than many in their community; only one (Ms. Green) had not completed high school; one (Ms. Trasket) had post–high school vocational training, and one (Ms. Smith) had an advanced degree. Three of the women lived with male partners (Ms. Smith, Ms. Afton, Ms. Blank) and two with other adult family members (Ms. Burns, Ms. Green), indicating a degree of stability in their personal lives. Only Ms. Smiley, who values self-sufficiency, and Ms. Powers, who appeared overwhelmed with her household of six children, did not have adult companionship in their homes.

Their responses to Family Reading workshops were similar to those of others who had participated in other schools as well as to those of prior groups of Central parents. They functioned as literacy learners, as literacy resources to their children, and as actors in the world. They served as program champions to others, helped in program dissemination both within the school and elsewhere and, in the case of Ms. Smiley, went on to serve in an important volunteer position in the school. However, there is no way of telling whether the home literacy practices of the mothers interviewed were more effective or more in depth than those of others whose home literacy practices were not investigated. Similarly, there is no way of telling from the data whether the mothers were more strongly oriented toward literacy at the outset than were parents who did not attend the workshops as regularly. As previously noted, work obligations prevented many from attending daytime meetings at Central School. Those parents may be equally motivated, but unable to participate. It would be incorrect and unproductive to assume they were not interested.

CHAPTER 8

Home and School Relationships

THE PORTRAYALS OF THE SEVEN WOMEN have shown us well-intentioned mothers concerned to do their best for their children. Although only a small sample, the interviews provide evidence yet again that parents in low-income, minority communities are concerned for their children's welfare and appreciate the help of the school. In this important respect, their responses to Family Reading resembled those of participants in other Partnership schools in Newark and in school-based family programs elsewhere.

As their initial motivation for attending Family Reading workshops, the seven women expressed the desire to "encourage" or "help" their children. In addition, all reported adult-centered reasons for their participation, notably the "enjoyment" and "interest" of the sessions themselves. They liked the participatory, welcoming nature of the workshops, the opportunity to interact with other adults, and the dedication and warmth of the teacher conducting the workshops. The dual motivation was often expressed in the same statement. Asked her reasons for attending the workshops, Ms. Blank said:

> It's interesting to me. Each time is a new experience, not just learning the same thing over and over. It teaches you different ways of reading to your kids.

All seven women reported learning about books and reading strategies and translating their knowledge into new behaviors with their children. All reported reading the workshop books to their children; some were stimulated to pick up new reading material for themselves; others reported that they had learned to improve their own reading skills.

Among the seven women, home-reading environments differed considerably, as did their personal styles, family background, household routines, and use of community organizations and other external resources. Manage-

94

ment of television, homework, and reading time, a factor in all households, was handled with varying degrees of regularity and strictness. Some mothers affirmed the educational value of children's programs; Ms. Smith compared television unfavorably with reading. The home of the one highly educated mother provided the most literacy-rich environment, but important variations not attributable to social class were seen among the others as well. Such variation tells us again that not all families in poverty neighborhoods are alike and warns against facile generalization about low-income, minority populations.

The diversity of home backgrounds included the admittedly rare presence of a highly educated, middle-class family in a poverty neighborhood. That fortuitous circumstance enabled consideration of what a middle-class parent might derive from the program as well as comparison with other mothers from the same ethnic group. Social-class differences may account for the fact that Ms. Smith, the attorney, was the only one to offer criticism of the educational process; the other mothers appeared pleased with the school as well as with the Family Reading program.

COMMONALITIES AND IMPLICATIONS FOR SCHOOLS

Commonalities as well as differences characterized the seven women. They were the mothers who came to Family Reading workshops regularly along with those who attended sporadically but out of no less a concern for their children's academic progress and a motivation to help. Ms. Smith had the additional goal of community betterment. The seven women are examples of how parents will respond to outreach by a school that welcomes them warmly and provides an engaging program. The fact that several attended Central School as students and all are long-time community residents may also have some bearing.

In the seven households, literacy activities had been conducted in a deliberate way prior to participation in Family Reading. What Family Reading did was to enlarge concepts of literacy and to broaden the scope of literacy behaviors. Because all of the mothers had been reading or telling stories to their children before coming into the program, Family Reading served to validate that practice and to encourage its continuation by providing books for home reading that were generally of a higher quality than those with which the parents were familiar. The greatest change, however, was the focus on reading strategies and discussion of books as supportive of adult development as well as of the children's developing capabilities. The mothers indicated that they had learned procedural knowledge of the discussion strategies that foster reading comprehension. They said they now understood the importance of strategic reading and used strategies and discussion techniques when reading books with their children. Ms. Afton's incorporation of Family Reading strategies into her home teaching system was a clear example of expanding a concept of literacy that had formerly been restricted to word knowledge and repetition. Parents (and to a great extent teachers) came to view literacy as an interactive thinking process rather than as a set of print skills only and learned how to operationalize the enlarged concept when reading to their children and in their own reading. Changes in belief patterns and adoption of actions based on new beliefs were major accomplishments of the program. They enabled participants to use the resources of discussion and strategic thinking to foster their children's reading development and help them to attain higher levels of reading comprehension necessary for school achievement and effective adult functioning.

As shown by the book service to which five of the mothers subscribed or by the early library visits, the mothers were willing to invest in literacy before Family Reading or formal schooling. Their responsiveness to the resource offered by a commercial service, the books by mail subscription, was particularly important in a community that has very few bookstores. The message of early exposure to literacy has become more generally known, although some Newark parents have still expressed surprise at seeing their preschoolers respond to books when attending a Family Reading session. Some aspects of the convenience and appeal of the commercial book service might be adopted by schools in sending library books home specifically for preschoolers, organizing book fairs, opening school bookstores, or adding a parent component to the school book clubs run by paperback publishers. Since parents everywhere ask for book recommendations, schools can promote home reading at an early age by providing short and frequent annotated lists together with information on how to gain access to the books.

The mothers interviewed described themselves as strengthening and supplementing school instruction. For example, Ms. Smiley felt that her reading sessions helped her son Dwayne when he was in preschool; Ms. Afton supplemented her daughter's preschool experience with her system for teaching letters and words; Ms. Burns assisted with spelling at the school's request; and when Morgana Smith could read and spell a number of words through using a kindergarten computer, her mother built on the school learning by providing books that the child could read by herself. Although not connected with school, Ms. Blank remembered teaching her son recognition skills and then being surprised when he picked out letters and words in the newspaper. Also on their own initiative, Ms. Smiley and Ms. Afton consciously created their own home-schooling systems for their young children. These mothers' self-assumed role of home educator goes far beyond that of homework helper, a familiar assignment running from school to parent, to embrace concepts of agency and partnership. The challenge for schools is to recognize and build upon the resources that these mothers represent.

The contributions of other household members also need recognition and inclusion in program planning. In addition to the mothers, the Smith and Blank fathers, the Burns grandmother, and the Powers older siblings read to the children. The Blank twins read to each other and to younger children. The Afton grandmother writes poetry and engages family members in storytelling. To be inclusive, family literacy programs need to reach out to all family members.

The literacy events spontaneously mentioned by the seven women as part of their typical day were book reading, skill practice, and storytelling. With the exception of Ms. Smith, none mentioned informal encounters with print that are embedded in daily activities such as writing notes or reading cereal boxes while eating. It may be that those more transient events did not register as important or that the Partnership's focus on book reading shaped their responses. Attention to environmental print was incorporated into several of the Family Reading workshops, however; notably, Tana Hoban's book of photographs of outdoor signs (*I Walk and Read*) was read in preparation for a walk through the neighborhood. Although other facets of literacy were not neglected, since teachers incorporated reading games, test-taking skills, and phonics reinforcement into the workshops, the Family Reading model emphasized comprehension strategies. At Central, when participants' interest in writing was revealed during their interviews, their pieces were shared during the workshops. Had their interest been known earlier, more could have been done.

Although it is clear that the mothers responded to the school's outreach, in considering the relationship between school and home we need to ask about reciprocity, that is, how the school program supported—or failed to support—the mothers' literacy skills and practices. There were several ways in which the school program failed to support home literacy. The influence of siblings as home literacy resources was not taken into account, nor was it clear whether the program utilized the mothers' preschool experiences as knowledge sources. Because neighborhood conditions precluded evening meetings at Central and other schools, parents who worked outside the community were effectively barred from participating in Family Reading workshops. With time and money in very short supply, other means of outreach such as home visitors or videos of the workshops were not feasible. Accordingly, schools such as Central could not reach a wider audience beyond the core "regulars" and perhaps 20 or so others who attended the on-site workshops. Although acknowledging multiple possibilities, this exploration of some of the practices of literacy in the homes of the seven women has shown them progressing beyond basic decoding and read-aloud fluency to the important next step of engaging their children in interactions characterized by high levels of cognition and enjoyable reading relationships. Literacy development occurs in multiple venues and multiple ways. Ethnographic studies such as Taylor and Dorsey-Gaines's (1988) research in Newark have documented the point that poor and undereducated people regularly employ literacy in their lives. However, levels and types of literacy use should be distinguished; using literacy only to identify letters or make lists is different from the reader-text interaction promoted by the Family Reading model (Snow & Tabors, 1996). Similarly, extensiveness of the recourse to print is important, since wide reading promotes vocabulary growth and knowledge. Home and school are primary agencies of socialization that in the past have operated as separate spheres. Family literacy programs have the potential to connect and enrich both.

MOTIVATIONS AND REWARDS

Further light on the Family Reading experience is provided by research that seeks to understand why parents become involved in their children's education. Hoover-Dempsey and Sandler (1997) have identified three major constructs that appear to influence parents' decisions to become and remain involved in their children's education. The first is parents' perceptions that both the school and the child want them to be involved. In the case of Family Reading, that welcome was conveyed by the enthusiastic invitations of the children, the warmth and perseverance of the project facilitator, and the sociability of the informal, nonthreatening workshop sessions. The mothers enjoyed and appreciated the opportunity to be with other adults. For example, Ms. Smith liked the sense of community, looking around and seeing that reading is "something we're all doing"; Ms. Powers liked the "sharing," the new activities she "didn't have as a child," and the chance to forget her problems for a while. Ms. Blank appreciated the fact that Family Reading workshops were different from school "because each session is a new experience, not just learning the same thing over and over."

Although school outreach is necessary for parent involvement, the researchers maintain that it is not sufficient, and that a second and third factor must be operating as well. The second is parents' sense of efficacy or the belief that they can exert positive influence on their child's education, which has been realized in Family Reading in the mothers' sense that they can transmit learning and enjoyment to which the children will respond. The mothers' ability to transmit their enjoyment of the books and to engage their children in discussion and interactive strategies appeared to be an important source of program validation. In other words, parents must perceive the program as working for the children as well as for themselves as literacy learners. An implication for family literacy planning is the need for instructional techniques, as well as content, to be consonant with the major program goal, that of fostering enjoyable reading relationships between adults and children. This economy of means and ends may be particularly important when planning small interventions such as Family Reading.

The third factor influencing parents' decisions to become and remain involved in their children's education is the parents' beliefs about their appropriate role. In some cultures, schooling is considered the domain of the teacher alone and parents do not consider themselves to be participants. As has been seen, quite the contrary was true of the seven mothers interviewed. Although it is not possible to pinpoint the time when the role of literacy resource began to seem appropriate, all seven of the mothers were in the habit of supplying their children with books from an early age. In the case of four mothers whose children attended preschool, it is possible that early education was a catalyst. Ms. Smiley, however, dates her resolve from the birth of her first child. Ms. Smith, the attorney, is again an exception; she describes learning about parents' educational role from child-rearing books, from general cultural knowledge, and from her mother.

Participants may extend their involvement beyond their own immediate families. In previous chapters, we have described parents who took Family Reading into their neighbors' homes or communities. In the small sample reported here there is also evidence that the mothers are functioning as actors in the world. For some it has meant being proactive toward the school; Ms. Blank borrowed school textbooks for her twins to read during the summer; she has also advocated for more Black history in the curriculum. Ms. Powers gave her phone number to her nephew's teacher and asked to be contacted if problems arose. Ms. Blank, Ms. Green, and Ms. Powers have actively reached out to friends and relatives in the community, encouraging them to attend Family Reading workshops. Ms. Smith has used her contacts with the other mothers to invite them into her church. In the case of Ms. Smiley, she has become involved in a large-scale effort to help other children and their families. Working in the school several days a week, she offers her services to all children who need individual help. "It's not just because of my own children," she said, emphasizing that she is responding to a need because many parents are working outside the home. Ms. Smiley keeps parents informed of her work with their children, and some parents have begun to call and ask her advice about schoolwork. She also has organized a parent center in the school.

Sometimes, however, a parent's educational role lies dormant until stimulated by an external event. In an earlier chapter, we saw parent involvement spring to life in the case of the mother who suddenly realized that her daughter had learned to read without her knowing it. Similarly, another mother attending a Family Reading workshop with her 2-year-old was surprised that he was interested in the books; she believed that her role in promoting literacy began when a child entered school. Although the mothers who were interviewed gave every indication of fulfilling an educational role as literacy resources for their children, Family Reading had helped them expand, rather than initiate, that role. Following Hoover-Dempsey and Sandler's (1997) line of reasoning, perhaps their regular attendance at Family Reading workshops was due precisely to that fact of role continuity.

Although none of the women mentioned their own reading improvement as an initial reason for participating in Family Reading workshops, all but one reported an increased interest in reading for herself or felt that her skills had improved. They also found the children's books to be interesting sources of new knowledge for both them and their children. Due in large measure to the supportive school program, these adults were functioning as literacy learners. Implications for family literacy are that goals may emerge during the course of program operations and that decisions about program content, in this case the literature selections, are important influences on motivation.

Supporting the adults' enjoyment and learning was the fact that the children enjoyed and learned also. In reciprocal fashion, both child-centered and adult-centered reasons were operating as motivational factors. The Central School program supported the mothers' literacy by reinforcing the importance of reading, teaching them ways of promoting comprehension, fostering family cohesion through enjoyable reading relationships, and providing access to books and human resources, as in the other Partnership schools. The way in which the program fostered literacy was by helping families to the next step of enlarged concepts of literacy that included discussion and strategic learning.

In describing an intergenerational program for nonnative English speakers, Paratore (1995) attributes the success of the program to its responsiveness to the needs of adults as well as children. Although the adults were interested and involved with their children's literacy, what kept them coming to class was "not only what they were learning about supporting their children's literacy, but also what they were learning about their own literacy" (p. 38). As with Hoover-Dempsey and Sandler (1997), this suggests that adult motivation must be addressed in school programs such as family literacy and that it is multifaceted. Connections must be made on more than one level in order to successfully maintain a program.

The relationship of personal enjoyment to cognitive learning and the power of literacy programs that are personally meaningful to the participants are obvious points but should not be minimized. In the case of Family Reading, it seems likely that these adult gratifications were a major factor in sustaining the mothers' initial motivation and keeping them coming back to the program.

THE FAMILY LITERACY HERITAGE

Like the middle-class families described by Taylor (1983), the mothers wove past and present together in talking about literacy as if to acknowledge that their early experiences set patterns for their family reading relationships now. As Leichter (1984, p. 40) suggested in her influential study, in this group of mothers, too, recollections of their own early experiences with literacy affected the attitudes and experiences they provided their children.

Memories of reading may be categorized by type of literacy activity. One such category is remembering books from childhood; that was the case of the three mothers who referred to a heritage of favorite books from their own childhood, such as Dr. Seuss and *Curious George* books that they have been reading to their own children. Hearing family stories, a second category, is illustrated by Ms. Powers, who carried on with her daughter the oral storytelling tradition she had enjoyed as a child, and by Ms. Afton, who continues the storytelling with her mother and sisters as well as her children. For both, the influence of their family of origin seemed particularly strong. A third category, the influence of reading role models, is explicit in the Smith home, where Ms. Smith transmits the literacy values of her mother, who continues to encourage literacy. In their enjoyment of the children's books and increased reading for themselves, the other mothers were of course acting as present-day role models for their children, whether or not they had significant adult models in their own childhood. A fourth category of literacy activity relates to family rituals; the Smith and Afton families' Bible sessions, the Afton family custom of sitting at the table reading aloud together, and the Blanks discussing the news are examples. The most common category, memories of being read to, are reported by all except Ms. Green, who was uncommunicative about her childhood, and Ms. Smiley. Finally, it is important to note that Ms. Smiley, who experienced neither book reading nor storytelling, responded to her family history too; with the birth of her first child, she "determined to be different." The past had influence in either direction.

How can family literacy programs benefit from knowledge about participants' literacy heritage? The first way is through recognizing that such heritages exist and honoring the individual by such recognition. The sharing of early reading memories in Family Reading workshops has helped participants to get in touch with childhood experiences that are still influential and has helped teachers recognize the various forms that those heritages can take. Such insights on the part of parents and teachers can help shape practices and strengthen learning with positive results in the present for both adults and children.

MULTIPLE PERSPECTIVES: THE FAMILY CONTEXT

Despite commonalities, Family Reading appears to have served the mothers in different ways and elicited the construction of multiple meanings. The families' lives differed from one another, literacy events took shape in varied family contexts, and the meaning of Family Reading for the participants differed as well. A first level of analysis was the identification of major themes expressive of this meaning.

In the case of Ms. Burns, Family Reading was seen as enlarging and enriching an existing routine. Ms. Powers, with her large and difficult household, regarded Family Reading as a way to take her mind off her problems; hers was "a hectic household with time for storytelling." For Ms. Smiley, "determined to be different," Family Reading helped her to raise her children in a manner much different from that she had experienced as a child. Ms. Smith saw "literacy in a larger context"; participation in Family Reading workshops was an opportunity to forward her mission of community betterment, and she regarded literacy as embedded in the context of wider life experiences, rather than as a special or unique activity. For Ms. Green, who said that "school is like a relative to me," the school and school programs were a haven, the place where she could make a contribution and be appreciated. Family Reading contributed to ongoing literacy events in the Afton home but the focus of the mother was on the importance of motivation. Ms. Blank, whose enthusiasm led her to declare that she would attend Family Reading workshops until her children were in Grade 8, saw the program as giving her a second chance to be an attentive mother. Her feelings resembled that of women in other Family Reading sites, some of whom had been school dropouts, who regarded the program as a second chance to relate to school in a productive way, and to parents who enjoyed reading books that they had missed out on when they were young.

On a second level of analysis, the multiple meanings of the Family Reading experience may be characterized as those expressive of continuance, transformation, and personal maintenance. Ms. Green and Ms. Powers appear to fit in the last category; both were seeking relief from personal difficulties. Ms. Powers expressed heavy dependence on the school as a resource for her role as home educators and as a distraction from her personal troubles. Ms. Green sees the school as a source of self-assurance, a way to maintain a sense of making a contribution. For Ms. Smiley and Ms. Blank, both of whom wished to change their prior histories, personal transformation and a different way of relating to others seemed imperative. Ms. Smith was intent on promoting social transformation through the Family Reading experience. The Afton and Burns households appear organized and serene with well-established literacy activities; new learnings from Family Reading are incorporated into family life, but without the intensity expressed by the others. They are representative of continuance.

The interviews also suggest some multiple meanings ascribed to the reading process itself. Most notable is the view of reading as a protective activity, as suggested by remarks made by Ms. Powers and Ms. Smith. Ms. Powers, worried about violence in the neighborhood and on television, was glad that her daughter was indoors occupied with a book instead. Ms. Smith, who apparently monitors her children's books in ways not possible with television, sees reading as protecting them from unsuitable material. "I know what the book is about, but I don't know what's coming on the TV," she said.

Other meanings of reading expressed by the mothers included reading as a way of showing love and care for children, especially at bedtime (Ms. Burns and Ms. Smiley), as a way to provide a quiet time (Ms. Green), as storytelling performance on the part of the mother (Ms. Powers), or as an occasion for reciprocal give-and-take between parent and child (Ms. Afton and Ms. Blank). These meanings were not exclusive; each mother viewed reading in a number of ways and all viewed reading as a way of engaging in an enjoyable relationship with their child. These meanings, however, contrast with the predominant meanings ascribed to reading in the school situation (reading as a tool, reading as a way of acquiring information) and may account for the disjunction that many children feel between their home and school literacy experiences.

One last example of multiple meanings highlights the differing perspectives of parents and educators as related to the interactive book-reading strategies. When describing their experiences using the strategies with their children, the mothers did not talk about deepening their own or their children's comprehension of text as a result of those processes, as a literacy educator might. Rather, they spoke only of the social meaning of the new procedures. Adopting the changed practice was meaningful to the mothers because it made reading more interesting and enjoyable, and promoted greater closeness with their children. Reading was no longer "just reading," but a process of social interaction. It seems doubtful that the cognitive and discussion strategies would have been adopted so readily if they had not served those purposes. The motivational weight of the interactive strategies lay in their consonance with the participants' deeply held values of family closeness.

IMPLICATIONS FOR READING PROGRAMS

For voluntary programs like Family Reading in which systematic intake and information about the adults' reading status is not feasible, interview studies such as this may be useful for program planning and for insight into the home literacy environment of students. Ascertaining and incorporating the parents' perspectives and needs is also important for program maintenance and recruitment; here the experience of a core group of program regulars can be instructive. In addition, as has been emphasized, investigating the parents' perspective is important if schools are to work effectively and collaboratively with parents in family literacy and many other endeavors.

Despite the schools' traditional focus on children as the beneficiaries of adult effort, equity and pragmatics call for attention to the role of literacy in the lives of adult family members, particularly those of women, who constitute the great majority of participants in family literacy programs. Attending to women's voices even in the partial social reality represented here can foster the democratic ethos espoused by family literacy programs.

From the interviews with the mothers, the Family Reading program has taken on a local habitation and a name. The personalization of the family literacy experience, the specific humanization, counters the assumptive thinking and stale stereotypes so often advanced about poor families living in the inner cities. Demonstrating the pervasiveness of intergenerational influence in literacy learning and its continuous operation, it challenges educators to learn from the family literacy heritages of families and to help them build on it in a more systematic way in the future. Beyond formal interviewing, sharing experiences, or asking questions in informal conversations are feasible ways that educators can reach out to families for the purpose of making those connections between home and school. The study has set out some of those questions. As tools to think with, the interviews also raise the issue of privacy and family boundaries. How much should educators try to learn about the family background of participants? To what extent would participants benefit if their contributions and strengths were more fully used as resources?

The study also shows what a small school program can and cannot do. It cannot address the larger social issues that impacted on the women's lives. For that, a comprehensive, integrated set of services is needed. It is important not to claim too much for any program. In the case of the mothers interviewed, Family Reading provided role continuity, rather than role change. The mothers were already reading to their children. What the program did was validate their home literacy practices by providing a social structure and recognition and by helping them to expand their concepts of literacy and go on to higher levels of the literacy process. Through its focus on enjoyment as well as instruction, the program enriched the literacy experiences of adults as well as children, and it is to be hoped that it will stimulate continuous engagement with books and reading. The fact that the family workshops represented meaningful learning to a highly educated, middle-class mother suggests that family literacy has benefits for a wide spectrum of society.

How do the multiple meanings illuminate one another? Although the facets of individual lives differed, perhaps most significant is the common theme that the social relationships promoted by the program were highly influential. In a sense, by developing feelings of community in the workshops and in interactive discussions with their children, the mothers enacted the social constructivist theory undergirding the program. For the mothers, a valuable meaning/motivation of the program lay in social relationships, and those social relationships facilitated their engagement with literacy and the valuing of literacy. For the teachers and myself as researcher the process began differently; literacy development was the goal and the social-support aspects more of a means to that end. Later, they came to be viewed seamlessly, as part of an integrated whole. Recognition of differing perspectives is another surprise of the teaching/learning process and part of its gratification. So is the recognition that perspectives can change.

CHAPTER 9

Teachers as Family Literacy Learners

I know how to talk to my second graders, but how do you talk to parents?

I was pleased to see so many parents are really interested in helping their children, and were just looking for an opportunity to do so.

I can't stay evenings; I have my own children to get to, my own family literacy to do at home.

It's been good getting to know more parents.

HELPING TEACHERS TO BECOME family literacy educators was one of the primary goals of the Partnership for Family Reading. The success of the family workshops depended upon the teachers who facilitated them. Although family literacy programs have proliferated in public schools in recent years, little training has been available to prepare teachers to function effectively in the new role of family educator (Shartrand, Kreider, & Erickson-Warfield, 1994; Shartrand, Weiss, Kreider, & Lopez, 1997). Yet teacher expertise is vital to those programs, because teachers are usually the carriers for more positive home-school relations (Epstein, 1987). Quite apart from the prompting of official directives, such as Goals 2000, Head Start, and Title I, or of professional standards such as those of the International Reading Association, most teachers and administrators have long recognized the importance of family involvement and want more of it (Chavkin & Williams, 1988). What has been less clear is the type of family involvement that school officials were willing to endorse and their preparation to do so effectively. The teacher who asked, "How do you talk to parents?" reflected the hesitations and lack of experience felt by many.

106

The Partnership for Family Reading was a field-based effort in which practicing teachers collaborated with a university researcher to develop and refine the knowledge, attitudes, and skills to inaugurate and maintain a family literacy program. For teachers, that meant adoption of a new role, that of family literacy educators, a change from their professional concept as educators of children only. Since the Family Reading workshops were conducted by elementary school teachers at the school site, the field-based setting raised distinctive issues of staff development and program implementation as well. Staff development was an integral part of the Partnership from its inception. In this action research project, staff development and program implementation proceeded concurrently, with program experience feeding back to enrich the staff development sessions.

PARTNERSHIP STAFF DEVELOPMENT

Staff from 34 elementary schools participated in the project over the years 1987–1995. Schools joined in successive waves beginning with 3 participating schools in the first 2 years, growing to 18 over the following 3 years, and to 34 thereafter. Because of the labor-intensive nature of Family Reading and because collegiality would foster program implementation, each school was asked to send a team of two or three educators to the staff development sessions. Participants included kindergarten and primary-grade teachers, librarians, teacher aides, curriculum coordinators, and several school administrators. Occasionally, mothers of students would attend. Out of a total of 90 individuals, all but 5 were women. The certificated teachers were experienced; about two thirds had been teaching for 16 or more years in the district and about two thirds had credits beyond the bachelor's degree. In response to an introductory survey, most said they were comfortable working with parents, whereas only half reported more than moderate familiarity with children's books or reading comprehension strategies. Fully three quarters of the participants were parents or grandparents themselves.

Guiding the design of the staff development were the following:

Goals directed to helping teachers
    learn Family Reading methodology
    establish comfortable relationships with family members
    participate in program development
    value and enjoy the program

Methods of experiential and participatory learning, characterized by
    informal workshop settings

modeling and hands-on activities
reading and discussing multicultural children's books
using interactive reading strategies
exploring issues in teacher-parent interaction
formulating implementation plans
sharing and networking
teacher presentations

Ongoing staff development, characterized by
    initial teacher workshops
    school-site consultations and technical assistance
    annual refresher and extension workshops

In the first 3 years of the Partnership, when the number of participating schools was still small, monthly sessions were held with the key Family Reading teachers. I was also able to coteach many of the family workshops and provide a model on site. Thereafter, staff development included an initial 3 days' training for new schools followed by two networking days each year for participants from all schools. The sessions were designed to help teachers establish a knowledge base about family-school relationships, adopt Family Reading methodology, establish comfortable relations with adult family members, and contribute to program development. Learning was facilitated by the supportive environment of the group sessions. Consultation on site and assistance in conducting the family workshops were also available.

Staff development was provided by myself, central office staff from the district, and, increasingly, by participating teachers. Teachers from approximately half of the schools have participated for 4 or more years, amassing considerable expertise. Overall, the staff development took an interactive research and development perspective (Griffin, Lieberman, & Noto, 1982; Tikunoff, Ward, & Griffin, 1975) intended to encourage teachers to take leadership in refining the program according to the local conditions of their respective schools (McLaughlin, 1990), to collaborate with other teachers, and to reflect on and evaluate their efforts. As the program grew and institutionalization in the schools took place, ownership of the program passed increasingly to teachers.

The Newark context for staff development contrasted with another area where Family Reading was then also being adopted, the San Diego (California) County schools.Through the efforts of the San Diego County Office of Education and in conformity with state mandates, schools there had already had the benefit of effective staff development in working with parents and many parent involvement projects were in place. Because of the prior experience, Family Reading seemed a natural addition to the process. Parents accompanied teachers to San Diego staff development sessions; lacking similar groundwork, Newark parents attended only at my urging. Also unlike Newark, the California schools used a literature-based and interactive approach to learning that was compatible with Family Reading. Although no adoption of a new program is without difficulties, these factors made the transition easier.

EXPERIENTIAL STAFF DEVELOPMENT

Educators have tended to assume that parents should adapt to school norms, rather than engage in reciprocal relationships. Another assumption has been that the role of the teacher is to remediate deficits and deficiencies that families may have, rather than to seek out and build on their strengths. Given the lack of preservice training and of experience working with adults in the school setting, how were those assumptions to be changed?

The way that was adopted was that of demonstrated experience. The hope was that teachers' experiencing the Family Reading workshops for themselves in an informal staff development situation and subsequently experiencing the gratification of working with adult family members would promote change in teachers' role concepts to that of family educators.

In the experiential staff development plan the major learning mode was participation in Family Reading workshops similar to those that the teachers would later facilitate for parents. The aim was to learn how to implement Family Reading methodology and to create an enjoyable learning environment. Following the Family Reading model, teachers first shared early reading memories with one another, then read children's books representative of different literary genres, engaged in cognitive reading strategies applicable to particular books, practiced those strategies with one another, and engaged in lively discussions of themes and generalizations about the books. The atmosphere was informal, open, and participatory. I served as staff development leader for the initial staff development sessions, modeling strategy use, guiding discussion and reflection, and helping teachers to build a knowledge base through updates on family literacy research and home-school relations. Collections of recent children's books were available at each of the sessions for teachers to browse through and evaluate.

As staff developer, my task was to model, think aloud, evoke, and guide participation, and to participate myself, including sharing my own early reading memories and enthusiasm for children's books. I described how my ear for language had been formed by my father's recitations of poetry at the dinner table (*The Charge of the Light Brigade* while we children ate our applesauce!) and about how the pictures in a book I was given, *Nancy Goes to Mexico* (author forgotten), stimulated wonder at the customs of another culture. Teachers told of their kindergarten experiences, of going to neighborhood libraries for storytelling hours, and of the books their parents read to them. The early memories helped us reconnect with parenting and being parented and the positive experiences of literacy.

In the next component of the workshop, I or one of the teachers would introduce a book representing a particular genre and model the reading strategy. For a book about a boy with an imaginary friend, the strategy of generating questions was used. I would display the cover and title (*In the Attic*) and, thinking aloud, say something like "I wonder why there are so many different things in this picture?" Participants would join in with questions of their own (Why is there a tiger in the picture? What's the boy doing there? What was in the attic? Does anyone live in a house with an attic? etc.). The idea was not to offer answers but to stimulate thought. We discussed how the strategy of question generation differs from the recitation routine of teacher question–student answer; teachers were to help parents generate questions of their own rather than pose questions for them to answer.

Employing the strategy while reading the book brought some answers and more questions as the teachers worked in pairs and then joined in group discussion. For example, participants commiserated with the "loneliness" of an only child, concluded that he was "spoiled" because he had so many toys, debated the merits of imagination and fantasy in a child's life, and disagreed with the contention that adults lacked imagination. In the process of reader-text interaction, they related the text to their own experiences and generalized from the text to more abstract issues. They also discussed the symbolism used and the extremely clever illustrations, pointing out that the sharp eyes of children were sure to notice all the details more readily than adults.

The book discussions were fascinating; no two sessions were ever alike. Teachers, no less than the parents, appeared to enjoy reading and discussing interesting children's literature and to benefit from the instruction in reading strategies and the deeper analysis of text that they involved. The children's books also evoked personal responses that were often indicative of cultural values. A book about bread evoked descriptions of the home delivery of fresh rolls from a teacher who lived in the Portuguese section of Newark, surprising the rest of us, who assumed that home delivery was a thing of the past. The next day the teacher brought in the basket she hung on her door each morning and the embroidered cloth used to cover the rolls, together with some samples from that day's delivery. The participatory nature of the staff development workshops and particularly the sharing of early memories relating to books, reading, storytelling, library visits, and recollections of one's own childhood set a relaxed and enthusiastic tone that pervaded the sessions.

In addition to providing experience with Family Reading, the staff development was designed to foster program ownership by the teachers. Reflective exercises during the sessions helped teachers identify the characteristics required of an effective family workshop facilitator. Reflecting on the staff development experiences, they identified such factors as knowing the participants, showing empathy, listening and not imposing one's own viewpoint, being flexible, evoking participation, and knowing the content of the children's books and the reading strategies. It was recognized, too, that teachers might not be able to enact all facilitator characteristics immediately. Rather, the staff development sessions provided a supportive environment in which concerns could be aired, new behaviors tried, and progress noted. In later sessions, teachers would try out the role of workshop facilitators and guide peers through a sample workshop.

During the staff development sessions, teachers collaborated to generate plans of action for their schools. They also worked together to create new workshop units using books and strategies of their choice. They presented the new units to the group; at subsequent sessions they described their experiences implementing them. Throughout the series of staff development sessions, the role of the expert was shared. Ownership of the program gradually passed to the teachers.

There was idea sharing throughout the sessions, with the end-of-year networking meeting being a particular occasion for teachers to share artifacts, anecdotes, and advice, to display photos and scrapbooks, and to describe the library trips, book fairs, and other creative activities they had added to the workshop model.

PRAGMATICS AND POLITICS

The pragmatics of program implementation came in for a great deal of discussion. Clear and engaging oral and written communication was necessary for good relationships with parents. Teachers shared and critiqued written invitations and announcements. Translations into the families' home languages were made available. The young teacher who felt comfortable with her second graders, but asked, "How do you talk to parents?" learned about her colleagues' experiences as parents and engaged in role play with them.

Teachers also helped one another develop realistic expectations about attendance at the family workshops and strategized for effective recruitment. They shared the realization that children, eager for their parents to attend, were energetic recruiters. For parents who could not come to school, many teachers arranged book borrowing for home reading and considered that a marker of participation. They also showed a willingness to work with whatever number of parents did actually attend. When only three mothers showed up for a session in a school that had recently joined the Partnership, the teacher overcame her disappointment and worked with them intensively; those three parents became enthusiastic promoters of Family Reading and the nucleus of a larger group. Recruitment of parents into the program was, however, a continuing problem, as with other voluntary family programs. A gradualist approach to building a constituency tended to conflict with the view often expressed by administrators that success was measured by large numbers. Several schools arranged early-morning or early-evening workshops to accommodate parents whose schedule did not permit them to attend school-hour workshops. Other schools simply did not have that flexibility.

Also of concern were the political aspects of school-site innovation. Planning time, access to duplicating facilities, space for the family workshops, and coverage of facilitators' classes while they conducted workshops were subject to negotiation, with varying results. Although central office administrators directed principals to give teachers time to plan the workshops, when other imperatives intervened planning time was forgotten. Teachers understood the need to reach out to parents in effective ways and complained about the lack of time in which to do so. Most administrators supported the program in tangible ways and some participated in the family sessions, but occasionally teachers had to resort to claiming the authority of their university partner to gain access to supplies. Some workshops were held in noisy cafeterias and one overcrowded school had to hold them in a public library down the street. Teachers learned to tolerate participants who did not come promptly at the appointed time.

The degree of forward planning and organization varied by school according to administrative support and the number of teachers actively involved in the planning. As might be expected, schools in which one teacher carried the load had a less extensive program than schools in which a team of three were active. In one such school, three teachers initiated the program for parents of children in prekindergarten through Grade 2, expanded to Grade 3 the 2nd year, and to Grade 4 the 3rd year. The existence of other, similar services in the school also made a difference, at least in the initial years of a school's adoption of Family Reading. For example, those schools that had ongoing community contacts, such as senior citizens groups that came into school to read to students, or community agencies and local businesses that provided services to the school on a regular basis, appeared to accommodate Family Reading more easily and to expand on the core activities more readily. Those schools, already being familiar with outside agencies and nonschool personnel, were able to build on their prior experience when implementing Family Reading. In other words, schools that had more resources, whether of personnel or experience, were able to do more.

At the district level, frequent personnel changes impacted on program continuity, as did increased demands on teachers and reductions in support services over the course of the Partnership. A favorable change was the district's adoption of a literature-based reading program to replace the skills-based curriculum after the 3rd year of the program. This more compatible approach permitted teachers to make strong connections between Family Reading methodology and their classroom teaching.

Of course there were surprises and insights to be gained. For example, eager to emphasize the importance of the teachers' new role as family educators, I was careful to remind them that the books and strategies were intended for use in the family workshops. Often, however, teachers would seize on a children's picture book with delight, exclaiming that their class would love it, or they would comment that they could use a particular reading strategy with their students. At first, I would hasten to remind them that what we were preparing were workshops for adults, not children. Their comments continued and finally I really listened to what they were saying. Naturally, teachers would want something that would connect with their classrooms—connecting a program with unfamiliar aims to the classroom teaching they valued was a powerful means of promoting an innovation's adoption. Moreover, the teachers were seeing the Family Reading staff development as a way to change from the skill-and-drill frontal teaching that they had heretofore had to use. They were seeing an alternative. Wasn't that something I also wanted? My concern over another sort of change had prevented me from seeing a desirable one that was happening in front of me. Eventually, changes in teachers' perceptions as educators of adults and families, not just children, would follow.

TEACHERS AS FAMILY LITERACY LEARNERS

For the teachers, the meaning of the Partnership experience was no less important than it was for family members. Setting out the perspectives of this important group of stakeholders illuminates ways in which they are vital to the operation of the program. From the inception of the Partnership, teachers' perspectives were studied through documentation of activities, settings, and self-reports. The school-based nature of the project and, particularly, the focus on teacher ownership, meant that practices would continue to emerge over the course of the project and differ by school. Accordingly, naturalistic methods were used to compile and analyze a database of field notes and videotapes of the staff development sessions, notes of informal contacts with teachers and parents, self-report surveys, and observations or reports of the family workshops in the schools. The aim was to understand human behavior from the participants' frame of reference, including that of the researcher (Bogdan & Taylor, 1975; Erickson, 1986).

From the teacher data, I identified themes relating to the value of the program, pedagogy, professional role, relationship with parents, and personal development. Meanings to teachers included the exercise of creativity through contributions to program development; enhancement of professional efficacy in the new role of family educators; role conflict as well as empathy on the part of those teachers who are parents; and the pleasure of positive relationships with other adults. Teachers' voluntary participation in the program, their implementation of the family workshops despite some daunting obstacles, and the longevity of their participation provide additional evidence that teachers valued the program.

CONTRIBUTIONS TO PROGRAM DEVELOPMENT

Teacher ownership and creativity was apparent in the many adaptations and enhancements made to the Family Reading workshop model. Among teacher contributions were the scheduling of trips to the public library so parents as well as children could get library cards; writing Family Reading newsletters; centering family workshops around holiday themes, such as Kwaanza; establishing special parent lending libraries in the school; and making parent-recognition ceremonies more elaborate, with special certificates, gift books, and speakers at the end of the year. Some adaptations reflected teachers' skills with puppet making and hands-on activities related to the workshop book, or expertise in storytelling and choral reading. Other adaptations showed Family Reading's adaptability to external mandates. When the district promoted coordinated teaching of reading and writing, parents in the workshops read family stories and then wrote some of their own, which were later featured at the end-of-the-year recognition ceremony. The characteristics of emergent writing were also covered to help parents understand that aspect of children's literacy development. Additionally, the district's program of parenting skills was strengthened in the many discussions of family life in connection with the workshop books. With regard to Newark's emphasis on testing, parents wanted to know how they could help their children do better on standardized tests. At their request, some schools incorporated instruction in test-taking skills into the

Family Reading workshop. Also out of responsiveness to parental concern, reading games for phonics reinforcement were included. The many new elements that were added to the model presented the challenge of negotiating between their value for literacy development versus their value for parent or teacher ownership of the program. Writing activities were a clear benefit in both respects, whereas some of the hands-on activities seemed tangential and time-consuming although enjoyable. These issues were considered at the staff development sessions as teachers shared experiences and often found focus through adopting one another's ideas. As program developer, I learned to appreciate the necessity of teacher ownership and to see it as one of the meanings of the program to the participants.

ENHANCEMENT OF PROFESSIONAL EFFICACY

The professional efficacy of teachers was enhanced through the extension of Family Reading methods in teachers' classrooms and throughout the school. An important meaning that emerged through teacher observation and self-report was Family Reading's function as a stimulus to other literacy activities in the school. For example, teachers in five schools initiated cross-age reading after learning of a program (Handel, 1995) in which Family Reading methodology was used by middle school students reading to younger children. Seventh graders in one of the schools, who had experienced Family Reading when they were in elementary grades, were not only using cognitive strategies when reading to first graders, but were also training classmates in the techniques. In addition, they were reading to younger siblings. Books used in the Family Reading sessions were circulated to classrooms to supplement reading activities there. One such book was so enjoyed that the teacher contacted the author, the children wrote letters, and the author responded by video, calling each child by name and responding to their questions. Although author contact is not uncommon in schools, this example was stimulated by a Family Reading book that may not have passed through the teacher's hands otherwise and the teacher regarded it as an extension of Family Reading.

Family Reading also meant changes in classroom teaching. All teachers indicated that participation in Family Reading had influenced their classroom teaching or activities with students, particularly with regard to the use of reading strategies. Responses indicated that teachers were using the strategies in their classroom teaching, some for the first time. Others were using strategies more often than before, or were more aware of strategies when using them, or felt more confident teaching reading strategies. Both they and the children enjoyed the interactive nature of the strategies. The particular characteristics of the Family Reading model may have been influential in promoting teachers' sense of efficacy. The model's format is essentially an instructional routine, in other words, a structure that was easy for teachers to learn, while accommodating individual creativity and ownership.

As teachers gained experience in the project, they demonstrated interactive strategies more readily in the staff development sessions as well. They were not always able to do so with parents, however, reverting to frontal teaching when faced with large groups or time pressures. Predictably, the open-ended discussion aspect of the program was the most difficult for teachers to adopt in both the staff development and parent workshops. In addition, questioning the text and helping others to generate their own questions was a strategy new to many teachers and seldom used before in the familiar setting of the classroom. As one teacher said, "I never thought to evoke questions from children; usually I ask the questions and the children answer."

Teachers also reported that they were reading more stories to their classes. Family Reading's use of interesting children's books as a learning vehicle aroused vocal enthusiasm and engagement. Teachers reported that they enjoyed reading books to children, but had not been able to justify their use in an educational setting before. They immediately began using them in classrooms as well as parent workshops. They also brought favorite books to the staff development workshops and shared them eagerly with colleagues. Affective, as well as cognitive, aspects of Family Reading methodology were shared.

The finding—serendipitous perhaps only to the researcher—that teachers adopted Family Reading methodology for classroom teaching meant that the staff development had served a dual purpose, with teachers recognizing and validating the use of interactive reading strategies and children's books in the classroom as well as in the parent workshops. That suggests that effective staff development for family literacy, or working with parents in other academic areas, should be connected with or adaptable to classroom teaching with students and should have some resonance with teacher beliefs. Articulation with a central value of the teachers was instrumental in involving them in the program; teachers valued children's books, but were unsure how to justify their use in the classroom reading program. Whether the impact would have been as great in a district whose teachers were less tied to basal readers and more familiar with cognitive learning and discussion strategies is an open question. What seems noteworthy is that teachers were able to adopt the new methodology for both family workshop and classroom learning, and that they began to create participatory learning environments even when the district was wedded to transmittal models of instruction. Another implication growing out of this

experience is that there is a need for teachers to perceive benefits for themselves as professionals, as well as for the children, in adopting a new methodology.

TEACHERS' FAMILY LIVES

Teachers extended the professional development resulting from Family
Reading into their own personal home lives. All teachers who were parents
took Family Reading books home to read and discuss with their children,
crediting the project with showing them new ways to establish enjoyable
reading relationships with their children. Others introduced Family Reading to their church or community groups. On the negative side, home responsibilities constrained teachers' willingness to stay after hours. As one
teacher put it,

> I can't stay evenings; I have my own children to get to, my own fam-
> ily literacy to do at home.

Thus although teachers who were parents integrated Family Reading into
their own family lives and expressed empathy toward the parents of their
students, they also experienced conflict between personal and professional
roles. Given the purposes of Family Reading, that conflict, which impeded
program flexibility, was particularly ironic.

POSITIVE RELATIONSHIPS WITH OTHER ADULTS

The personal pleasure that teachers took in their adult relationships with
parents and colleagues in the program also seems important in view of
the typical isolation of the elementary classroom teacher. Family Reading
workshops and the collaborative planning that they entailed helped miti-
gate that isolation. The pleasure built into the program content through
the use of interesting books and an informal atmosphere in which to discuss them extended out to color and enlarge teachers' relationships in the
school setting as a whole.

Participation in Family Reading influenced teachers' relationships with
colleagues, causing them to engage in greater sharing and collegiality.
Teachers reported sharing ideas and working together in the program in
their respective schools and enjoying the collaborative effort. They pointed
out that joint, rather than individual, efforts were needed for program success. Some teachers reported serving as resources for colleagues who
wished to know more about children's books and reading strategies.

Teachers found their relationships with parents a source of gratification as well. Familiarity and competency as a family educator was suggested by changes in teachers' relationship or attitude toward parents. Teachers felt that they had successfully recruited parents into the program, learned how to make them welcome in school (made "the parents feel the school belongs to all of us—children, teachers, parents"), established "a partnership" with parents, and facilitated their engagement with reading and other subjects. Contributing to feelings of efficacy were teachers' reports of greater knowledge of children's literature to share with parents and increased confidence in public speaking, which they believed heightened their competencies in the eyes of parents. One teacher said:

> The parents see me as having another role and believe I can provide a wealth of knowledge in assisting all family members to read, be motivated to read, and have better comprehension of what is read.

All teachers reported more interest in the adult family members and enjoyed the pleasant, informal contact in the family workshops. Many saw for the first time that parents wanted to be involved in their child's education. They were pleased to note instances of parents' seeking further education for themselves, enrolling in other literacy programs, or serving as school aides or volunteers as a result of the program. Teachers also felt that they had learned about the families' home life and culture and saw their students in the context of home as well as school.

Significantly, too, teachers saw changes in the parents. They felt that parents showed greater understanding of teachers' work and of teacher-student relations and were more confident and comfortable in the school setting. Teachers felt that parents now viewed them as "really concerned about helping . . . not just givers of homework." Teachers enjoyed getting to know the parents, and appreciated the parents' enthusiasm and interest. The personalized nature of Family Reading workshops was often cited as a reason for the changes. "Parents have gotten to know me on a more personal level and feel more comfortable to approach me in asking for aid" was a typical response.

Reciprocal relationships between teachers and parents emerged. When parents began to ask for book recommendations for their own reading, teachers reported pleasure in this new experience and recognition of their professional expertise. They also reported sharing their own home-reading experiences with parents in the workshops. Changes of perspective occur with contact, as Epstein found in her research on teacher attitudes toward parents (Epstein & Becker, 1982). It is likely too, as the teacher efficacy research suggests, that teachers' increased confidence in their own abilities to relate and work with parents helped shape their positive response.

Commonly, however, impact on children conditioned teacher attitudes toward adult family members. Teachers valued the program for the delight expressed on children's faces when the children knew that their parents were in school for the adult workshop and would read to them afterward. Conversely, an ongoing concern and source of discouragement for teachers was the lack of participation on the part of some parents.

When teachers worked with parents who appreciated the program, they learned firsthand that undereducated parents were concerned for their children's welfare, that the adults' progress could enhance their own sense of professional efficacy, and that closer contact with the parents of their students could be a source of pleasure that did not compromise professional expertise, the last in accord with findings that interaction leads teachers to take a more favorable view of parents (Epstein & Becker, 1982). Reciprocally, teacher practices can exert an important influence on parents' concepts about their educational roles and ways in which to become involved in their children's education (Epstein, 1995; Epstein & Dauber, 1991). As has been seen, the practices of Family Reading facilitators enabled them to influence parents in positive directions, which is indeed the rationale for the work of helping teachers learn to take on the role of family educators.

Less successfully addressed by the program was the issue of what teachers can learn from parents. As family literacy research indicates (Morrow & Paratore, 1993, p. 198), the prevailing mindset appeared to be that parents learn from schools; there was less attention to developing the reciprocal relationship in which schools and school personnel might learn from families and parents be considered resources for the school. However, teachers did indeed report learning from their observations of parent-child interaction and gaining insight into the earnest desire of parents to help their children. In the parent workshops, they heard family stories, noted customs and beliefs, and learned about home-reading practices. Teachers encouraged parent volunteerism in their classrooms. They were aware that low-income, minority parents might be intimidated by the school setting and worked to make them comfortable. Consonant with the Family Reading model of active involvement of learners, teachers made earnest efforts to evoke participation during the family workshops, and did not regard parents as merely an audience. Teachers' openness to response and initiative suggests a willingness to learn from parents.

Recognizing that the adult family members have enhanced their own literacy and learned something important about their role in fostering the literacy development of their children, teachers appear to have grown into an expanded role as family educators.

CHAPTER 10

Reflections on Gender, Class, and Race

THE BROADER SOCIAL REALITIES of gender, class, and race were reflected in the Partnership for Family Reading and in the lives of its teacher and parent participants. The limitations of poor schools in poor neighborhoods conditioned many aspects of the project despite the earnest efforts and competencies of teachers who served as Family Reading staff. Again using data from the project as tools to think with, in this chapter I discuss issues of gender, class, and race as they impinged on the Partnership participants.

GENDER AND FAMILY LITERACY

Looking at the Family Reading workshops, it was hard to avoid the impression that reading was a gendered activity. The workshop facilitators and virtually all the family members in attendance were female. In Central School's sessions, 3 of the 25 to 30 participants might be male; in less well-attended sessions the lone man who occasionally appeared was much welcomed. Most of the books used in the program accorded with women's interests or centered on family relations; although male and female children were equally represented, there were few adult male characters. The workshops made a special point of fostering sociability and connections among participants, which some believe is a female relational style. Occasionally, the workshops have included sessions on ethnic dress and hairstyles at participants' requests.

The extent of reading as a gendered activity is also suggested by the literacy heritages described in the interviews. All of the reading memories involved the respondents' mothers and none described a father's influence. That could only strengthen the feeling that literacy is a female domain with which men need not be involved.

Finally, the gendered nature of the Partnership for Family Reading was apparent in its effects on teachers. With its focus on nurturing relationships, Family Reading articulated with the gendered nature of elementary school teaching as women's work. That connection was illustrated by teacher-parents who brought family reading books into their homes, and who occasionally brought their own children to Family Reading sessions. Because of their particular content, family literacy programs are especially likely to evoke, if not influence, the family lives of program providers as well as learners. Teachers, most of whom live with children, are no exception. Examples from the Partnership are both negative and positive. Participating teachers in Newark, all but two of whom were female, reported demands on their time and lack of flexibility because of home responsibilities, commenting that they could not do workshops after hours because "we are parents, too, and our own children are coming home." A kindergarten teacher, anticipating joining her own three-year-old twin daughters at the end of the school day, added, "Another part of my day is just beginning." On the positive side, all teacher-parents took Family Reading books home to read and discuss with their children, most crediting the project for showing them new ways in which to establish reading relationships with their child. In her study of teachers who are parents, MacDonald (1994) has noted the interweaving of this dual role, and finds the same situation of mixed responses to its demands.

Connectedness of life roles can be deeply satisfying, and nurturant relationships are surely a good thing for both teachers and parents. Women and men in many occupations besides teaching are puzzling today over ways to integrate work and home life and how to prioritize their multiple responsibilities. What is difficult in the case of Family Reading, as in family literacy programs generally, is that since the people involved are so predominantly female, the roles of nurturance and connectedness will be assigned all that more firmly to only one gender. Increasing male involvement in family literacy would not only demonstrate the generality of those roles and their value to men, but would benefit women by freeing them to explore other aspects of their family and professional lives.

In family literacy programs, the well-substantiated finding that children's school achievement is most strongly correlated with mothers' level of education (Sticht, 1992) can operate as a two-edged sword. On the one hand, it has lent urgency to efforts to enhance women's educational levels; on the other, such efforts may involve unrealistic expectations and pressures to perform. As is evident in the current political climate in the United States, social policy affecting poor and minority people often blames the victim, particularly if the targeted population is composed predominantly of women. Family literacy programs may be no exception to this situation. Programs in schools that focus on children as the beneficiaries of adult effort rather than on service to the adults themselves are particularly likely to blame low-literate parents as uncooperative or to overlook the needs, strengths, and contributions that they can bring to school programs.

THE PREDOMINANCE OF WOMEN

Usually, the gender factor in school programs is disguised by the use of the term *parent, family member,* or *caretaker* to designate participants, terms that present a genderless version of reality and preclude identification of relevant issues. What difference—if any—does it make that the vast majority of learners and instructors are female?

The first point is the necessity for women to be involved in programs that improve their literacy status, given the proportion of women in poverty and the mandates for workforce participation that are being demanded of welfare recipients. Improved literacy increases their chances for economic self-sufficiency. In addition, the strong correlation of mothers' educational level with children's school achievement makes women's participation vital to interrupting the intergenerational cycle of low literacy.

More negative implications are pointed out by Cuban and Hayes (1996), who warn that programs may diverge from and thereby subtly denigrate home literacy practices of the women participants. That may be particularly likely when programs adopt a school-to-home transmission stance (Auerbach, 1989) and fail to consider home conditions and cultural practices. Such programs may overlook mediating mechanisms operating at home, such as the influence of other family members, on the assumption that clear and simple causality runs between mother and child. As a result, gender roles and the various ways that families may be organized are not likely to be questioned.

Programs that fail to account for gender run the risk of overlooking issues of particular concern to women, such as domestic violence and health needs, or of failing to foster the group interaction and relationships that are many women's preferred modes of learning (Kazemek, 1988). Sometimes the curriculum reflects gendered norms that shortchange women. Potts (personal communications, October 31, November 15, 1996) points out that activities may change from those involving discrete skills to those in the conceptual domains when men are present. For example, women are taught discrete skills of nutrition and meal planning, but men are offered training in planning as a form of higher order thinking. Potts sees this as a failure of understanding on the part of predominantly female staff.

Cuban and Hayes (1996) also warn against a caretaker orientation in programs that do not account for women's multiple roles, and against reinforcing the stereotype of reading as a feminine activity. Although there are exceptions, such as the family math programs offered in conjunction with family literacy at some schools, the lack of numeracy learning at many family literacy sites also reinforces gendered norms, as Cuban and Hayes point out (p. 9). Since reading materials serve as models of social practice, books selected for family literacy programs need to be evaluated for gender as well as race and class fairness. Interestingly, although children's books have more male than female child protagonists, mothers are depicted more often than fathers, perhaps on the assumption that mothers will be the readers (R. Ludeman, personal communication, November 5, 1996). Finally, focusing on women as "conduits of literacy" implies that women pursue literacy education to "meet the needs of others and are the first access point in the literacy circuit rather than the subjects of their own learning" (Cuban & Hayes, 1996, p. 7), a danger that requires careful negotiation in many family literacy programs regardless of model.

On the family level, participation in a literacy program brings change to the family system, and change does not always come easily. In addition to positive factors, such as more shared reading in the home and pride in achievement, change may also bring conflict. Research evidence indicates that this is the case for women in particular. Their new role as learners may not be easily consonant with their multiple responsibilities as caretakers and job holders, causing resentment on the part of their children, as well as of the men in their families. The independence and assertiveness that education involves are counter to gender norms in many communities. When the woman's emerging status is threatening to males in the family, the disapproval of the men and pragmatic obstacles may impede participation. Increase in abuse and domestic violence may occur, and in literacy settings such abuse may serve to silence women (Gowen & Bartlett, 1997).

THE PARTICIPATION OF MEN

Although greatly underrepresented in family literacy programs, men do attend. Their participation is much appreciated by program providers who recognize the importance of male involvement in children's education, as well as the literacy needs of the men themselves. Male participation is usually viewed as something "special"; as one teacher put it, "They added flavor to the conversation."

Those men who did participate in the Family Reading workshops at Central School had regular contact with their children whether or not they lived with the family. For example, the Smiley child's father has come to the workshops at the request of his enthusiastic son. Given men's responsiveness to their children, one way to involve men in family literacy programs is to run programs that arouse enthusiasm among the children and encourage the children to convey that to their male as well as female parent. Using the child as a communication link may be the most practicable way for schools to reach male parents who are in contact with their children but do not live in the household or maintain contact with the school, as in the case of the Smiley and Green families. Even Start programs and those of the National Center for Family Literacy report a similar influence of children's urgings upon adult, although not necessarily male, participation.

In the Smith, Afton, and Blank households, where men were present, the men attended the Family Reading workshops although by no means as often as the mothers. However, participation in a child's literacy learning does not depend on attendance at school functions, and literacy activities in the home are not confined to Family Reading. The entire family participates in the Bible readings in the Smith and Afton households and Mr. Blank reads with his twin son and daughter. Against these hopeful indications is the larger demographic issue of the underrepresentation of males in inner-city communities. In impoverished areas where unemployment is high, one in four adult African American men are estimated to be under the jurisdiction of the criminal justice system, either jailed or on probation. In a few localities, prison literacy programs help men to maintain communication with their children through book sharing (Genisio, 1996). However, the social disorganization represented by these demographics call for resources beyond the capacity of family literacy programs alone.

Just as provision for child care and transportation have been recognized as essential enabling factors for women, evening classes facilitate participation for men. For example, about one quarter of participants in a Massachusetts program are male, attending mainly in the evening (Paratore, 1995); night classes on Native American sites are roughly 50–50 (Potts, personal communication, July 24, 1997). Special events on weekends also draw male family members. In addition, among some immigrant and Native American groups, their greater facility with English may explain a higher than usual percentage of male participants.

As traditional primary caregivers of young children, mothers have been the subject of many research studies dealing with their role as early teachers. Much less information is available on the father's contribution to children's early literacy development. However, in this era of dual-earner families and the growing number of single fathers, men are becoming more active in child rearing and are being encouraged to take a more active role in their child's education, as books and articles on fathering and efforts by the literacy field itself attest. This social trend provides an additional justification for male participation in family literacy programs. Testing that hypothesis in a study of Mexican American fathers, Ortiz (1996) found that those men who shared child-caring responsibilities with their wives tended to engage in more literacy interactions with their young children than did men in families with traditional gender-role division. He attributed that to the fact that, already assuming child-related duties, those fathers could easily incorporate literacy interaction into their established routines. Marital roles regarding child rearing were a more important factor than social class or age in his small sample.

The implications of social change leading to greater male participation in family literacy programs are intriguing. One can imagine recruitment publicity showing fathers reading newspapers with children or pointing out environmental print as they walk them to school. Certainly more children's books featuring fathers in nurturant and literacy activities need to be available. Female encouragement helps, too. Potts (personal communications, October 31, November 15, 1996) reports that mothers and aunts often encourage husbands, sons, brothers, and nephews to attend family literacy sessions, and others report success with special "men appreciation" events. Not to be overlooked is encouragement from the children. There is every reason to believe that like fathers in the Newark program, men will be delighted when their children ask them to participate.

Ortiz (1996) reports that fathers want to be involved when given opportunities to do things that they consider appropriate. Many fathers do engage in literacy-related activities at home upon which programs can build. Reading about sports, calculating batting averages, reading occupational material and recreational print on board games, as reported in Taylor's (1983) study of middle-class White families, are among the many possibilities. Father, mothers, and other adult relatives need to be asked what they wish to do and to contribute to program development.

The extent of the social change in child-rearing practices is not clear and is likely more common among middle-class families. Nearly half of African American and Latino men earn less than the poverty level and low male earnings reduce the likelihood of marriage (Levine & Pitt, 1996). With almost one quarter of the nation's children living in father-absent homes, the need for male participation in family literacy programs is acute.

Researchers report social constraints on men's decisions to participate. In the inner city, African American fathers want relationships with their children, but find their role complicated by lack of financial resources (Gadsden & Smith, 1994). Many men in the study did not understand the relevance of their engagement with literacy either for themselves or for their children; with their limited exposure to good schools, they tended to vacillate between hope and distrust of school-related agencies. Nonetheless, if literacy is considered a lifelong process, rather than being limited to school years, family programs may be able to engage their participation. In addition, since children in the low-income and single-parent homes described may have interactions with relatives and other men who are not their biological fathers, outreach should extend to those other significant male figures.

There are no easy solutions to the issue of male participation, particularly among low-income and minority populations. However, family literacy programs are not alone in trying to involve fathers. On the state and local level many agencies are reaching out to men, including noncustodial fathers in poverty areas, teen fathers, and single fathers, with parenting-skills training and other services; in a few instances, linkages to their children's education are included (National Governors Association, 1998). Family literacy programs should seek out and collaborate with those agencies in their communities. Rays of hope emerge also from the family literacy programs that have identified facilitating factors, and these have seen fathers and their children benefit from their attendance. The Newark program, for example, has seen fathers who work the night shift come to an early morning Family Reading session, breakfast on a cup of coffee and a roll during the workshop, and then with great joy read to their children (Handel, 1992). Grandfather, older brothers, and husband-and-wife couples have also attended. Women can help involve the men; so can children. Parenting styles can differ and women staff members may need training to work with men, while still presenting a gender-fair program.

ISSUES OF CLASS AND RACE

Residents of poverty neighborhoods are not bereft of cultural capital. As the interviews with the seven Central School mothers indicated, they have literacy heritages, use whatever resources the community provides, and draw on the school as a major resource. The contrast case of Ms. Smith, a professional woman, suggests differences in concepts of literacy that are probably attributable to social class. Ms. Smith regards reading and writing as normative activities, embedded in family life and taken for granted as one of several important things to do. The other mothers tended to regard their book-reading practices as something special; with great pride they recounted their book purchases and their bedtime routines with their children. In discussing her childhood, Ms. Burns said that she prized the rare occasions when her mother had time to read to her. Will the children today remember Family Reading as something out of the ordinary—as a special practice rarely duplicated? Or, as is hoped, will the orientation to literacy come to seem normal, a result of continuing home support and successful school experience? Whatever the practice, how will the children build on it? Will the memory of books and questioning and discussion be there as a resource to be tapped in later life? That is surely one of the hopeful aspects of family literacy.

Another important issue raised by Ms. Burns's comment on her mother's involvement is how much intervention is necessary for later achievement—and for whom. There are example of adults who grew up in unpromising circumstances crediting one outstanding event or individual for their later achievement, as did Richard Wright, who said that hearing the story of *Bluebeard* as a child released his imagination and set him on his path as a writer. Perhaps such people are the exceptions, individuals with personal strengths, luck, and the ability to use or create the opportunities they need. There are also examples of adults growing up in the most favored circumstances who because of personal characteristics or inability to take advantage of opportunity do not amount to much. The contrast between Ms. Smith's and Ms. Burns's perspectives on reading points to large and unsolved issues in educational practice and human behavior.

Just as statistical correlations document the impact of poverty on the practice of literacy, so the social mileu of the Newark schools and neighborhoods have constrained the operations of the Partnership for Family Reading and the lives of its participants. Drug addiction, weapons at the high schools, and street violence, sometimes at the door of the elementary school, have limited opportunities and diverted energies for learning. One of the mothers, Ms. Powers, framed the issue on a personal level. Concerned about violence in the neighborhood, as well as on television, Ms. Powers felt upset when her kindergarten daughter asked her why people kill other people. She did not know how to explain the conflict between home and school values and the dangers of the street, and was glad that books and home life would shelter her young child for a while. The challenge for schools and family literacy programs is how to make learning meaningful under such conditions and how to help strengthen families so they can withstand and work to change the exigences of poverty and disorder. Schools and small programs can contribute to this effort, but cannot be maximally effective alone. Integrated services on the community level supported by community action and public policy on the state and national levels are needed. In the early days of the Partnership for Family Reading, a teacher asked, What about the parents who are hooked on drugs? How will we reach them? I explained that the program was not intended to deal with problems of that magnitude—our resources were insufficient. Then, my answer seemed satisfactory; we were busy trying to get the program under way and many family literacy programs in the 1980s had a similar perspective. It seems insufficient now.

The individuality of the mothers at Central School counter invidious stereotypes of poor African American women in the inner city. One of the purposes of the interviews was to highlight the individualities and varia- tions within a minority group. Yet racism, that given of African American life, must affect them all. Ms. Blank must campaign for more books on the African American experience to be included in the curriculum, and Ms. Smith, who has strong feelings about transmitting her ethnic heritage, re- counted an incident that made her understand the complexity of her ef- forts. Ms. Smith had asked her son, an artistically talented child, to illus- trate *Ebony Locks*, the African American version of *Goldilocks* that she had written. To her dismay, he drew a picture of a "nice little White girl" copied from another book. Conventions of the majority culture had shaped his drawing, rather than attentiveness to his mother's story or observation of people around him, including his own younger sister. Scott-Jones (1997) has pointed out that even affluent African American parents must teach their children to negotiate the experiences of racism in our society. How much more must the parents of Central School, confined to a school district poor in resources and a high-poverty neighborhood whose dangers were articulated in several of the interviews.

Within the school setting, the Family Reading facilitator, Ms. Conti, is seen as fostering an appreciation of many ethnic groups, including African Americans, and helping parents to understand the variety of cultures through discussion of multicultural books.

Ms. Conti, who is White, and the librarian, a woman of color, have often collaborated in the workshops, but Ms. Conti was the leader and was perceived as such. Although she is well liked for her personal warmth and for her role in Family Reading, the affection she evokes may present dangers of its own. Reading the interviews in a different way, I wondered whether the mothers were developing loyalty to a school that was failing the students. Central School has a poor record of student achievement. During the years of the Partnership, the school was not able to manage the behavior of students in the upper grades. Praise of Ms. Conti was well deserved and Family Reading was a bright spot. I am not suggesting that the school would be better off without it. All of the participants liked and benefited from it. But Family Reading was an improvement from the inside that had minimal effect on the school's overall functioning. Was the reli- ance on Family Reading's facilitator keeping parents from challenging the system, perhaps mounting neighborhood efforts for school reform, or in other ways taking a further emancipatory step? What is involved here is the issue of growth, the ability to promote action beyond the boundaries of a small-scale program.

Ms. Blank criticized the lack of African American books in the school and worked to make that curriculum change, but of the mothers interviewed, only Ms. Smith engaged in a thoroughgoing critique of educational practice. Of the mothers, only Ms. Smith had options; the following year, she removed her children from Central and enrolled them in a private school. Public schools are particularly important institutions in high-poverty neighborhoods where other community agencies may be limited or unstable. That makes it all the more important that those who rely on the public schools as a social and academic resource have opportunities to evaluate and change them.

CHAPTER 11

Small Wins and Large Circumstances

> A small win is a concrete, completed, imple-
> mented outcome of moderate importance. By
> itself, one small win may seem unimportant.
> A series of small wins at small but significant
> tasks, however, reveal a pattern that may at-
> tract allies, deter opponents, and lower resis-
> tance to subsequent proposals.
> —K. E. Weick, "Small Wins"

FAMILY LITERACY PROGRAMS have accumulated some "small wins" in the
face of large social circumstances of poverty, educational underachievment,
poor schooling, and discrimination. Family literacy is not a solution to
those problems. Higher levels of literacy alone will not reduce poverty,
improve poor schools, or end discrimination; they may not even promote
great achievement in the educational system. What family literacy programs can do is equip people with the motivational and cognitive tools
to address those problems. Questions of program organization, program
ownership, the literacy content of programs, and staff development for
family literacy raise issues on the path to that goal.

THE PARTNERSHIP FOR FAMILY READING—
GOALS, EVALUATION, IMPLICATIONS

The goals of the Partnership for Family Reading were to improve the reading competencies of both adults and children, and to help teachers achieve
a role transition as family literacy educators. As an action research project
in family literacy, the Partnership was subject to the multiplicity of vari-

ables confronting family research as well as the multiple circumstances of a large and complex school district. The participating families varied in range of ages of the children, household composition, and prior child-rearing and reading practices of the parents. The extent of adult participation, the number of workshops attended, could not be controlled in this voluntary program. On average, adult participants attended three workshops per year. In-depth ethnographic data documenting the ways in which the program effected reading practices could not be obtained, although there were solid indications that both quantity and quality of home reading increased and that teachers were regarding themselves as instructors of adults as well as of children. As with Epstein and Dauber's (1991) study, Partnership teachers experienced more positive attitudes toward parents as their contact with them increased.

In considering the methodological question of what type of assessment made sense for a minimal-intervention program, I have followed Weiss and Jacobs's (1988) recommendation for a broadened notion of program evaluation that takes into account the specific and differing nature of programs and that does not evaluate solely on the basis of impact. In considering the variety of effects that programs can have en route to their overall goals, I focused on the adult participants in the program, out of the belief that their perspectives, often overlooked, were vital to understanding program effectiveness and the influence of gender on program operations and policies.

In general, I adopted Weiss and Jacobs's (1988) five-tier approach to evaluation for small programs in which the evaluation process consists of needs analysis; accountability (documenting the implementation and participants' needs and responses as described in Chapters 4, 5, and 6); program clarification or formative evaluation (a continuous process throughout the program); and progress toward short-term objectives (as described in Chapters 6, 8, and 9). Given the Partnership's limited resources, a fifth component, program impact involving a large-scale, research-oriented effort, was not feasible. Perhaps, as suggested by Weiss and Jacobs (1988), "evidence of accessibility, use, and satisfaction" was "all that is possible and all that should be required" in a program such as the Partnership for Family Reading (p. 62). The teachers' willingness to assume the new role of family literacy educators, the evidence of parents' increased engagement with literacy particularly at higher cognitive levels, and the spread of the program throughout the school district attest to use and satisfaction with Family Reading.

The program's multiple meanings as derived from the perspectives that the mothers and teachers brought to and developed from the Family Reading experience suggest the productiveness of investigating the meaning of the program for its participants. Investigating the place of literacy in a daily routine with children, practices of storytelling or book reading, personal literacy heritages, parents' and teachers' relationships to one another and to the school, concepts of literacy, and the effect on classroom teaching and home reading are illustrative of the practice of viewing families and teachers as sources of information and literacy learning (Gadsden, 1994). The portraits of the mothers also showed inner-city African American life as far more diverse and complex than aggregate descriptions indicate. In so doing, they put a human face on the large social problem of poverty and underachievement.

Sustained participation in a voluntary program such as family literacy requires strong motivation and conviction of the program's importance despite possible unfamiliarity with the work of literacy learning and the stresses of daily life. Although adults may participate because they foresee economic benefit from additional education, their strong desire to help their children, often reinforced by the children's enthusiastic encouragement, is the primary motivation. This synergistic relationship is one of the strengths of family literacy.

Looking at a different population, African American adolescent mothers, Neuman, Celano, and Fischer (1996) found that literacy was considered important because it served as a tool to address economic and social concerns. Findings such as these articulate with and add an additional dimension to what Auerbach (1995) describes as a multiple literacies model of family literacy, one that puts participants' culturally specific practices and ways of knowing as the centerpiece of curriculum (p. 653). They also demonstrate again the variety of possible perspectives on the part of family literacy participants and the importance of investigating and building on them for program development.

Ascertaining and incorporating the parents' own views and needs bears directly on program maintenance and development; in the Partnership the experience of a core group of program regulars was instructive. As many in the field of home-school relationships have insisted, understanding the families' perspective is necessary if schools are to design effective curricula and to work collaboratively with parents. For example, Delgado-Gaitan (1992), in her study of Mexican American communities, points out that educators needed to know that the parents were providing physical and emotional support to their children, but were "perplexed" when help with academic tasks was required. If parents came to school requesting clarification, teachers helped them and believed that those were the parents who cared. With the benefit of understanding their students' home learning environments, educators could reach out and provide systematic access to needed resources and "communication linkages that enhance schooling opportunities" for students and their families (p. 513). Again, the message for family literacy and partnership programs generally is that schools need to take the initiative in reaching out. The other side of the equation, the perspectives of teachers and other service providers, is also vital for effective, collaborative efforts.

The major finding emerging from the Partnership is the importance of program articulation with deeply held values of the participants—family closeness in the case of the parents, and story reading as a source of enjoyment on the part of the teachers. Honoring those values provided a basis on which to build other effective program components.

Several implications for practice may be drawn from the Partnership for Family Reading experience:

1. Programmatic content is important for maintaining program commitment. Written materials must be meaningful to adults as well as children; they serve as vehicles for critical reading and reflection.
2. In school-based programs particularly, teachers need to view adults as individuals in their own right, not merely as instrumental in their children's development. The concept of parents as self-directed learners should guide program activities, as should the concept of teachers as learners in a collaborative enterprise with family members.
3. Instructional methodology may need to be negotiated and opportunities should exist for alternative practices. Not all teachers or parents support the social constructivist view of literacy embodied in Family Reading, and in today's political climate some school districts may actively oppose it.
4. The labor intensive nature of the program means that staff need time and experience to become effective with the methodology. Without solid administrative support, teachers may become preoccupied with program logistics, rather than focusing on instructional activities.
5. Establishing enjoyable reading relationships between children and adults and between teachers and parents is a prime benefit of the program; when necessary, other considerations should be subordinated.

PARTNERSHIPS AND PROGRAM OWNERSHIP

The new vision of partnership between families and schools has implications for program ownership and content. As seen in the Partnership for Family Reading, teachers and parents brought changes not anticipated in the initial workshop model.

In contrast to the traditional hierarchical organization of schools, partnerships involve agreement on common goals and relatively equal status among the stakeholders in terms of the resources, capacities, and power that they bring to the relationship. In business and the professions, collaboration among adults may be the norm, but in many schools it is unfamiliar, although welcome, as the Partnership experience again shows. School resources are often limited, and opportunities for interaction are constrained by school schedules as well as by home and work demands (Moles, 1993; Swap, 1993). Busy teachers may use their expertise to tell parents what to do or to set tasks that reinforce schoolwork without truly sharing authority or drawing on the expertise of the parents. Asking parents to review spelling words or sending books home for them to read are examples. It is not that such practices lack value; rather, they represent a limited perspective of home-school relations in which school personnel alone define goals and activities, using a school-to-home transmission model to shape the relationship. On the other hand, asking participants to be collaborators as well as learners in a family literacy program may invite confusion initially, particularly if they are accustomed to looking on teachers as authorities. In those cases, the wiser course may be a gradual implementation of an inclusive model that draws on the strengths and resources of family members and views teachers as learners as well as experts.

The pragmatics of experience tell us that people whose personal history has left them wary of the educational process will be more committed to learning if programs harmonize with their beliefs in some way and afford them feelings of self-enhancement and pleasure. Parental beliefs and concepts about literacy, which are often based on parents' own childhood experiences, affect their interaction at home with their children as well as their relationship with external institutions. Parental beliefs play a part in the choice of informal activities at home; for example, across cultures, reading aloud to children may or may not be a social practice. Formal teaching by parents of decoding or other basic skills, as with some of the mothers interviewed, usually reflects their beliefs about literacy and their own role in fostering it.

The issue of congruence between parental beliefs and practices on the one hand and schools and family literacy programs on the other needs to be negotiated. Whether a reflection of their own schooling experiences or limited use of literacy consequent on their educational level, discordance between parental beliefs and programmatic aims presents a problem for family literacy programs that seek to involve parents in the education of their children.

It is not uncommon that participants' beliefs about literacy learning are at odds with instructors' theories. For example, the educator may focus on meaning-based activities, but the adult learners may view literacy as essentially "learning and mastering the orthographic code" (Goldenberg, Reese, & Gallimore, 1992, p. 529). That was the experience of some parents in the Partnership for Family Reading who requested that phonics activities be included in the workshops. In schools throughout the country, parents have protested against developmental or "invented" spelling in early grades, skeptical of the theories of emergent literacy and whole language on which the practice is based. Although decoding is certainly important, the narrowness of the definition possibly reflects not only the nature of the adult learners' schooling, but also a failure to identify as literacy oral language and other communicative activities experienced in daily life. That may be due, in turn, to a distinction between schooling and "real life," a bifurcation that may be realistic, since in many cases the schooling of people in poverty may have seemed unrelated to their home culture or to opportunities for work or self-development as an adult.

A strong theme in adult education is that participants should be co-constructors of their own knowledge. This theme is grounded in Paulo Freire's emancipatory philosophy, which states that learners should control the content of their learning and how it is taught, and in principles of adult development that involve freedom to choose one's goals. Yet here there are cautions about instructor allegiances. Gowen and Bartlett (1997), in discussing a workplace literacy situation, pointed out that the instructor's attempts to enact the participatory principles of Paulo Freire were not accepted by the African American women participants; they preferred working alone, were largely silent, and resisted politicization of the curriculum as well as activism.

In a study of Latino families, Goldenberg, Reese, and Gallimore (1992) recommend adapting the family literacy intervention to the beliefs of the family. That may be an excellent initial strategy through which to build trust. Family literacy is a process, however, and beliefs can change. In a project with another Latino population, researchers found that participants themselves rejected the skill-and-drill workbook lessons that they had originally requested as examples of good teaching (Shanahan, Mulhern, & Rodriguez-Brown, 1995).

All low-income and minority families face challenges. Ideally, programs should help them meet challenges, not exacerbate them. One type of family with extraordinary challenges are those with special needs children. As Harry (1996) points out, in those cases it is particularly important that intervention supports rather than disrupts adaptive processes already established by those families.

Adolescent parents are another population with distinct and special demands. Neuman, Hagedorn, Celano, and Daly (1995), concerned that existing intervention programs have had little success and have often failed to understand the culture of the adolescent parents served, first interviewed 19 African American teen mothers from low-income backgrounds to elicit their perspectives on child development, learning and literacy. The mothers were enrolled in a school-district-sponsored literacy program and their toddlers were in day care near the school site. Then, based on data provided by the teen mothers, programmatic modifications were made.

The aim of the study was to incorporate the mothers' beliefs into the educational programs, thereby establishing a collaborative relationship between families and professionals. The mothers' wish to monitor their children's progress and to become positive role models led to arrangements for their greater involvement at the day care center. The day care staff helped the mothers link their own literacy learning to activities with their children and taught them how to become actively involved. This change resulted in a "delicate shift in the balance of power" between staff and families (p. 822) and the empowerment of the teen parents to participate more effectively in their children's education. The Neuman study strongly suggests the importance of obtaining perspectives of the learners in order to build effective and collaborative family literacy programs.

Auerbach (1989), protesting the "deficit hypothesis" that she said informed many family literacy programs, advocated a social-contextual model that builds on families' cultural strengths and addresses their life concerns. Similarly, Cochran (1987) advocated an empowerment concept that assumes that individuals understand their own needs better than others do and that individuals should have the power both to define their needs and to act upon that understanding (p. 107). These views have considerable implications for family literacy programs in terms of power relations, curriculum, and goals. They imply that participants, in partnership with instructors, should create and enact the family literacy curriculum, that instructors must be cognizant of the life circumstances and culture of the participants, and that both should put literacy into the service of social change. On these grounds, Auerbach (1989) strongly criticizes the "school-to-home transmission" model, which valorizes school practices and overlooks the many literacy-related practices that are ongoing in the homes of low-income and minority families.

Auerbach's criticism has been influential. Current programs more in line with Auerbach's thinking use a multiple literacies model or a social change perspective. The former acknowledges participants' culturally specific practices regarding literacy and uses that knowledge as the "centerpiece of curriculum" even if it is "incongruent with educators' own pedagogical understandings or preferences" (1995, p. 653). The social change perspective incorporates, but goes beyond, culture to emphasize issues of power. Here the focus is on changing institutions and addressing conditions that cause marginalization rather than on changing families (Auerbach, 1995; Taylor & Dorsey-Gaines, 1988). Parents' advocating for more Black history courses in the school curriculum or lobbying legislators for funding for a battered women's shelter are examples. Dialogue, content centering around key issues in participants' lives, and action for social change are key elements. According to Auerbach, many programs incorporate some of these elements, but few are premised upon them entirely.

Auerbach's work is with family English literacy in a university setting. In her analyses, she does not distinguish between the variety of settings for family literacy and their respective characteristics and constraints—an omission that seems ironic given her focus on contextualization of literacy in the learners' home culture. Nor is Auerbach's criticism of school-to-home transmission universally accepted, as the experience of Shanahan and colleagues (1995) indicates. Many minority and immigrant families regard mainstream and school-based literacy as the route to success; researchers Delpit (1995) and Edwards (1994) argue strenuously that minority parents should not be denied instruction in the skills and practices that have helped middle-class children achieve in school. Again we are faced with the reality of multiple pathways to literacy, multiple uses of literacy, the need for sensitivity to context and beliefs, and an awareness that programs evolve and change, as do their participants—instructors and learners alike. And the voices calling for empowerment are cogent reminders that the ultimate good of literacy is to enlist it in the cause of social betterment.

CONTENT OF FAMILY LITERACY PROGRAMS—WHERE'S THE LITERACY?

Decisions about the content of family literacy programs are complex, relating to concepts of literacy goals and how to promote them as well as decisions about relative emphases on adult and child literacy, reading relationships among family members, and the myriad emotional, social, and economic ramifications of family life that affect and are affected by literacy development and that might be addressed by programs. Family literacy programs range from small community programs focused on book reading, to school-based programs grounded in research such as the Partnership, to comprehensive programs such as Even Start and the National Center for Family Literacy programs that involve participation for many hours per week. In the recognition that literacy is embedded in many life situations, comprehensive programs have included instruction relating to physical health, nutrition, emotional well-being, child development, access to community resources, and other family support services. Increasing collaboration between the literacy and health fields has meant more accessible health information and the resulting opportunities to use it in literacy programs. The Kenan model of the National Center for Family Literacy from the beginning incorporated parenting education, an umbrella term for topics such as those listed above; parenting education is also mandated by Even Start. Evaluations of both large programs have shown a greater retention rate of participants compared with other groups or compared with situations in which participants were faced with an array of services provided by separate agencies (Philiber, Spillman, & King, 1996; St. Pierre, Swartz, Murray, & Deck, 1996). With continued participation comes the opportunity for continued learning. It has been suggested that these family literacy programs are more likely to retain participants because several members of a family are engaged in meaningful activities at the same site and the mother of a young child does not have the problem of making alternate child care arrangements, a point particularly relevant given women's predominance in family literacy programs.

On a higher level of administrative coordination, integrated delivery of family support services has been held out as an efficient and cost-effective model. Integrated services provide for more basic needs of the entire family such as legal and medical services, access to public agencies, and job counseling and employment services, together with the academic and parenting components. The Rochester, New York, Family Learning Center, for example, provides all of these services together with early childhood and adult literacy education at the same site.

An issue that arises with the provision of multiple services is the linkage between literacy and the other program components. To what extent is literacy linked with the coordinated services? Does an integral connection exist? Are literacy materials used or created during informational sessions on parenting, for example? Are the literacy requirements of a job search made clear? Is literacy used as a tool for understanding forms, applications, and medical instructions? When weight control and diet was a concern for one Even Start group, the instructor was able to make a linkage with text material right away. Should linkages occur at every stage of programs or do programs need to meet participants' basic survival needs first? Certainly literacy should be seen as relevant to adults' lives and concerns, but focus on the centrality of text without attending to pressing life needs is likely to be counterproductive. Just as hungry children have trouble concentrating on schoolwork, so adults facing problems with housing or personal safety find it difficult to focus on literacy improvement. Service providers need to exercise flexibility in pursuing these issues and to devise ways to use literacy as a tool to address them. A danger exists that literacy will be slighted in programs of coordinated services. The extent to which the literacy focus can be augmented in integrated and coordinated service programs is a challenge that many providers face.

If the family is the unit of interest in family literacy programs (Nickse, 1990), it is by no means clear that family literacy programs are directed to the entire family. Although other family members may be brought in, as in the Hackensack C.A.R.E.S. program described in Chapter 2, the focus is on the mother-child dyad. The ways in which to study effects on entire families rather than only on immediate participants are time-consuming and expensive beyond the means of typical programs and many research organizations. Nor is there a clear theoretical base with which to guide the study of literacy functioning within entire families. To some extent, the field has been able to avoid this difficult issue because of the high percentage of single heads of households among program participants. However, not taking into account all the children in a family or not exploring the influence of extended kin or other influential adults results in a necessarily incomplete picture for the purposes of both practice and research.

The complexity of serving an intergenerational population and definitional difficulties in the concept of literacy itself complicate the evaluation process. Which literacy processes are to be evaluated and what are the criteria for choosing them? Is it sufficient to do separate assessments of adult and child progress, or is the family the unit of analysis and, if so, how should it be studied? What relative weight should be given to measurable literacy improvement as compared to life skills, attitudes, and expectations that may serve to foster literacy? What weight should be given to improvements in economic status or employment? The new federal and state work mandates put pressure in that direction and are changing the shape of many family literacy and adult education programs.

Taking into account the wide variations in the intensity and quality of Even Start programs, the National Center for Family Literacy (NCFL) sponsored a 1997 study of only those sites designated to be of "high quality," according to the Even Start criteria of the provision of intense, continuous, and integrated services. The study reported solid academic gains for parents and children who had participated in those high-quality programs. In studying only the "best" programs, the research reinforces the National Even Start Evaluation recommendation (St. Pierre et al., 1996, p. 18) that quality improvement for the Even Start program as a whole is needed in order to make a substantial difference in tested results. Whether there will be resources and capacity for such a broadscale improvement is an open question. One factor that may contribute to capacity building is the requirement that each Even Start site conduct a local evaluation of its progress and needs. Participating in a systematic analysis may raise awareness and stimulate problem solving on the part of the service providers. Implementing needed improvement, however, is likely to involve the deployment of additional resources, and the availability of those resources depends on the political economy within which, in common with many smaller family literacy programs, Even Start and NCFL programs operate.

Influencing program decisions and the evaluation plans based on them is the need for realistic planning for the financial and human resources to support the program. Alignment of resources, programming, and evaluation has to be an ongoing process, particularly in the case of family literacy programs that are dynamic in their responsiveness to their participants' emerging and sometimes unexpected needs and situations. Variety among programs and changes within a program that reflect the fluctuating needs of its participants preclude the use of prepackaged curricula that cannot be modified or that lack a theoretical grounding to guide modifications (DeBruin-Parecki, Paris, & Siedenburg, 1997).

STAFF DEVELOPMENT FOR FAMILY LITERACY

Family involvement and family literacy are not yet central topics in teacher education programs on either the undergraduate or the graduate level. The relative paucity of curricula reflects the fact that only 26 states mention parent involvement in their teacher certification requirements; moreover, those requirements are typically defined in vague or superficial terms and may include the teaching of academic or parenting activities themselves, rather than of how to work with parents to enhance those skills (Radcliffe, Malone, & Nathan, 1994; Shartrand et al., 1994, 1997). Special education and early childhood certifications are most likely to include the parent involvement requirement. Only six states mandate coursework or competency requirements in home-school relations for school administrators (Radcliffe, Malone, & Nathan, 1994) which is particularly unfortunate given the leadership role expected. The degree to which teacher and administrator requirements include home-school relations with regard to reading is not known.

Several states, however, have taken other initiatives to promote home-school connections and family literacy. In 1988, California led the way by mounting a comprehensive state policy to support parent initiatives, including family literacy training for school personnel and ongoing in-service staff development in many districts.

One guideline for staff development seems clear: experiential staff development and experience in the field are powerful means of learning. In common with the Partnership, at least one national study (Shartrand et al.,

1994, 1997) recommends the use of experiential models for professional development in working with families. In a study of an immigrant Spanish-speaking community, Allexhalt-Snider (1995) pointed out that teachers with prior experience in working with parents or other community members had built a base of knowledge that assisted them in interacting with students' families during fieldwork in a college course. She recommends that such experience be provided for undergraduate teacher candidates who lack it. Other examples of experiential preparation at colleges and universities include classroom-field-classroom sequences. In one such course, graduate students spent 4 weeks on campus developing curriculum guides and evaluating materials, 6 weeks delivering on-site ESL instruction to parents, and 3 weeks in reflective debriefing again on campus (Bermudez & Padron, 1987). Another long-running graduate course begins with developing a knowledge base about family issues, proceeds to clinical work involving the tutoring of children with learning problems, leading parent discussions, and preparing parents to take over the tutoring; and ends with students creating additional family involvement projects intended as contributions to the field (Evans-Schilling, 1996). Self-reflection and awareness of diverse cultural values are built into both courses, as is peer support. An after-school tutoring program for children provided the context for a fourth university program; after a 6-week preparation phase in literacy theory and the role of the parent in developing children's literacy, undergraduate and graduate teams tutor the children, instruct parents in reading techniques, and mentor and coach the parents as they practice the techniques during reading and writing activities with their children (Herrmann & Sarracino, 1991).

In an early childhood project described by Baker, Serpell, and Sonnenschein (1995), teachers learned about home literacy practices from parent diaries. The parents of preschoolers kept records of literacy activities and an inventory of literacy opportunities in their households.

Edwards (1994), a university researcher, described a program at a rural elementary school in which reciprocal learning took place. Primary teachers who were enrolled in an on-site course became informed about family literacy and culturally diverse home environments that were similar to those of their students. Offering an instructional medium for the parents, they also modeled book-reading strategies on videotape. Parents critiqued the effectiveness and clarity of the teacher tapes, thereby providing teachers with the powerful message that low-literate parents could contribute "insightful information to classroom teachers" about ways to help parents share books with children (p. 199).

At Montclair State University, a workshop course in intergenerational reading partnerships prepared teachers with knowledge about family literacy and required them to pilot a family involvement project in their school. Teachers were helped to negotiate their initial uncertainty about doing something "different" in their school; they were taught strategies of involving colleagues in their project, and course participants served as resources for one another throughout. Projects ranged from parents visiting classrooms as "mystery reader of the week," to parent-child book discussion clubs, science literacy projects, and developing a resource book for parents of children with learning difficulties.

Other examples of university courses with strong experiential components include fieldwork to implement family literacy in schools as part of a public service course, and a reading methods course that includes service learning in hospital clinics in which undergraduates model reading techniques for parents. Clinical practica on the master's level may include communication with parents, and students might present one or two workshops, but there is little evidence of in-depth work with families (Laster, 1996). Most often, family literacy is offered as part of traditionally taught courses in reading or elementary education, with the extent of its treatment driven by an individual faculty member's particular interest in family literacy and home-school partnerships. However, at least one university reading program has transformed its clinic into a family learning center, and at least one other university has instituted a family literacy course as a requirement for the students in its master's in reading program.

Professional development in family literacy has been offered in many school districts, notably those in San Diego County, California, which have adopted and adapted the Family Reading model in conformity with its more general emphasis on home-school involvement. The National Center for Family Literacy conducts an extensive training program in its Kenan model at its Kentucky headquarters and throughout the country for those Even Start, Head Start, and other personnel in schools.

Model standards for preparing teachers to work with families have been promulgated by national, state, and professional organizations. They address developmental competencies for beginning and experienced educators. As analyzed by Chrispeels (1996) the policy documents define expectations for teachers' working relations with families such as knowing and valuing the communities and cultures represented in the school, using that information in working with parents and students, providing parents with strategies for assisting their children with learning activities at home, and two-way communication with family members. To these expectations, primarily student-centered, the Parent Involvement Framework for Teacher Training of the Harvard Family Research Project (Shartrand et al., 1994, 1997) adds expectations that school personnel will involve families in decision-making and will support families' social and educational needs.

Another point about staff development needs to be emphasized, that of the reward structure for teachers participating in family literacy programs. As Shartrand and colleagues (1997) point out, teachers, "who are often overworked and face many unrealistic demands, need to know how family involvement can benefit rather than burden them" (p. 59). In the Partnership for Family Reading, the rewards of mutually supportive relationships with families were experienced by the teachers. These rewards were largely intrinsic, the satisfaction from doing new and demanding work that expanded their professionalism and dedication to others. Stimulated by their experience, some teachers went on to other special projects or more advanced academic work. Recognition of their efforts by school administrators and the university was forthcoming, but in informal and unsystematic ways.

For family literacy programs to become established in a school district on a continuing basis, it is likely that a school mission statement relating to parent involvement or family literacy would have to be operationalized on several administrative levels, including that of teacher evaluation. Chrispeels (1996) describes how the California State Education mandate on parent involvement as reflected in one district's mission statement was operationalized as specific indicators of teacher effectiveness. Using several state-specified teacher evaluation categories (student progress, instructional techniques and strategies, professional responsibilities), the district constructed indicators of teacher effectiveness in communicating and working with parents in each category. The policy instruments, together with staff development and other activities, have been used to foster parent involvement and increase home-school communications. According to Chrispeels (1996), the failure of many districts to address policy goals in the teacher evaluation system may send a "mixed-message to teachers about the importance the district places on parent involvement" resulting in lack of quality in programs and uneven implementation, since communicating with families would be left up to each individual teacher's discretion. In addition, clear evaluation standards would have the benefit of protecting teachers from being evaluated more by "parental complaints than by positive and proactive work with families" (p. 195).

Another factor that has relevance for evaluation of family literacy as well as more general partnership programs is the quality of instruction in a school district. Looking at student achievement in inner-city Baltimore schools that had school-home-community partnership programs, Epstein, Clark, Salinas, and Sanders (1997) found that although the programs had boosted attendance and achievement rates beyond that which would have been predicted from previous years' data, achievement rates remained quite low in comparison to state standards. Partnerships by themselves were not a solution to the problem of poor academic achievement. Although they added something, "it is excellent classroom teaching that will be needed to dramatically improve students' writing, reading and math skills" (p. 4). Quality of instruction makes a difference.

Policy initiatives, the experience accumulated by existing programs, and the dedication of practitioners and researchers who champion family literacy give hope that teacher preparation in this area will grow. For the families typically addressed by family literacy programs, effective teacher education is particularly needed. Above and beyond the usual issues of distance between the institutions of school and home, missions must be redefined, staff development in adult learning must be provided, and strategies for working with adults who are experiencing a great deal of life stress need to be developed. Schools that are themselves poor in resources must be helped to develop the capacity to reach out to families.

This analysis highlights once again that no one program or intervening factor is a solution or quick fix to multifaceted problems. In the case of family literacy, improved classroom instruction for students may magnify and sustain the positive motivation and academic skills that parents in family literacy programs impart to their children. Improved quality of instruction in family literacy programs themselves may enhance the development of both children and parents directly. As Scott-Jones (1993) points out, poor schools compound the difficulties of poor families in low-income communities. Broadbased school reform is necessary. The nested contexts within which family literacy and other programs operate not only increase the difficulty of program evaluation, but, more important, remind us of the need for concerted action in many areas. Programs such as family literacy appear to be necessary but not sufficient for large effects. To meet the large challenges of poverty, low literacy and reduced life chances, improvements along multiple dimensions may help convert "small wins" into larger ones.

CHAPTER 12

What's in a Name?

In New York City, there is no longer a Department of Welfare; the new name is the Family Independence Center and local offices are now called job centers. The welfare caseworkers who used to work in those offices still do but now they're called financial planners. Throughout the country the word "welfare" is being excised and agencies re-titled to emphasize the necessity of work. The New Jersey welfare department is now the Department of Workforce Development; the Massachusetts Department of Public Welfare is the Department of Transitional Assistance; Florida's welfare program is now the Work And Gain Economic Self-Sufficiency (WAGES) Program; the new name for Texas' welfare program is the Workforce Commission and in Michigan clients go to the Family Independence Agency.

—*New York Times*, July 5, 1998

THE ASSUMPTIONS AND IMPLICATIONS of the welfare name changes are readily transparent. The new names send a powerful message to the poor: Welfare's safety net is gone; in 6 months or 2 years (depending on your state of residence) you will have to find a job, find someone to support you, or simply, somehow, get by. Legislators who have enacted the new regulations know they have constituents who feel dismay at the idea of multiple generations of recipients, or who view single mothers on welfare with distaste, or who lack sympathy with the concept of welfare itself; for them, the new terminology provides reassurance that things have changed. Whether they have changed for the better is an open question. Whether the reduction in caseloads since the 1996 change in federal welfare legislation was due mainly to the discouragement of potential clients and whether applicants have been integrated into the workforce successfully and at a living wage is as yet unknown. As for the people formerly known as welfare recipients, in many parts of the country they are now designated "job seekers." While many welfare recipients have been job holders in the past, often on a part-time or temporary basis, and are seeking jobs with living wages now, the notion of calling everyone, including a single parent with a young child and no visible means of support, a job seeker borders on the absurd. Furthermore, that individual already has a job, taking care of a young child.

IMPLICATIONS OF WELFARE POLICY

The political purposes that contributed to the development of family literacy programs were apparent in the movement's beginnings; then the goal of remedying an intergenerational cycle of underachievement was considered important to the economic and social health of the nation. Now, public policy has begun to exert urgent demands that family literacy and adult education programs accommodate to the realities of welfare reform. The Personal Responsibility and Work Opportunity Reconciliation Act of 1996, which dramatically changed federal welfare law, has diminished the position of education as a means of helping people move from welfare to economic self-sufficiency, despite the fact that recipients with stronger educational skills are likely to become self-supporting more quickly. Putting primary emphasis on work, the new law mandates 20 hours per week of work or workfare community service for single parents, sets time limits on welfare benefits, and restricts opportunities for involvement in education. Under the federal law and state regulations, the long-term benefits of education in enhancing quality of life and the positive correlation between income and educational attainment are secondary to the imperatives of having job readiness and employment, no matter how low paying, as soon as possible. In a comprehensive analysis of the welfare-to-work initiative, D'Amico (1997) points out that postsecondary education may be needed for individuals to attain stable employment with prospects for advancement. She maintains that if the policy goal is savings in the welfare budget, cheaper, short-term programs may result in some employment but no real change in participants' lives or economic advancement. If self-sufficiency and personal success is the goal, public investments will be costly and long term and require education tailored to personal needs of participants.

One provision of the new law that does recognize the value of education is the requirement that teen parents receiving welfare benefits remain in or return to school until they have a high school degree or the equivalent from an alternative educational program. Teen parents and their children are at high risk; almost 80% of the children born to unmarried high school dropouts live in poverty.

State regulations implementing the federal welfare mandate vary. Some states require welfare recipients to find work immediately; in others, recipients have a 2-year period before benefits will be cut off. Some states permit participation in adult education to count as part of the required 20 hours of work per week, but most states do not. Those states are reporting declines in enrollment in adult education programs (D'Amico, 1997).

The work requirement is likely to fall most heavily on women. For single mothers, fulfilling the work mandate and also engaging in educational programs may be logistical impossibilities due to time constraints and the need for child care. Lack of transportation and distance between the work and education sites may be additional obstacles. Moreover, as D'Amico (1997) points out, single mothers are likely to need more education, not less, if they are to earn enough to afford child care and adequate health insurance for their families. That assertion is substantiated by an analysis of Los Angeles County showing the mismatch between the literacy levels of mothers on welfare and the skill requirements of the local labor market; even those who are able to find work will not earn wages that lift their families out of poverty (Levenson, Reardon, & Schmidt, 1997).

In states where education counts toward the work requirement, it is expected that programs will see an increase in applicants with very low literacy levels and troubled life circumstances; those with somewhat higher levels of literacy are more likely to find community service or entry-level jobs that may or may not lift them out of poverty (D'Amico, 1997; Potts, personal communications, October 31, November 15, 1997).

Although many adult education programs have included family literacy in the past, family services are receiving particular attention now as part of an initiative to recast and reinvent the practice of adult education. Spearheaded by the National Institute for Literacy, the reform agenda, Equipped for the Future, is building curricula to foster the goals of adult learners for achievement as citizens, workers, and family members (Stein, 1997). The danger is that pressure on adult education to focus on the mandate for employment may displace attention from the equally valued arenas of citizenship and family.

From the perspective of the learner, as indeed from that of many literacy researchers and providers, literacy is interwoven with the fabric of life in a holistic way and is not a set of skills or abilities limited to specialized circumstances. The inseparability of literacy learning from the contexts of learners' lives is summarized by D'Amico (1997), who demonstrates how child care, health needs, and poverty condition women's opportunities and how violence and abuse affect their ability to engage in literacy classes or to maintain employment. Adult learners in the Equipped for the Future study defined broad goals for themselves in their roles as family members, citizens, and workers. These multiple goals, rather than literacy for economic purposes alone, are shared by adult educators who must decide how and whether to participate in initiatives directed toward the jobs strategy "while maintaining a personal and programmatic commitment" to a broader view of the purposes of literacy (D'Amico, 1997, p. 53). It is a conflict between the short-term goals of the welfare-to-work initiative and commitment to the long-range purposes of education.

A similar perspective with specific reference to family literacy has been expressed by Gadsden (1994), who says that programs

> must be developed around a set of assumptions about children and family learning that is not limited to a desire to break the cycle of illiteracy, but that also enables family members to construct useful meanings and definitions of literacy that advance the goals, aspirations and expectations of the adults and children within the family unit. (p. 79)

Auerbach (1995), decrying the tendency of advocates to hold out family literacy as a solution to economic problems, warned:

> Focus on the unit of the family as the locus of change precludes consideration of social, economic, or institutional forces which may constrain family life and impede literacy development. (p. 650)

The relationship between low literacy and poverty is mediated by a complex of societal factors. Although low literacy may be more prevalent among the poor, and more than 80% of participants in family literacy programs have been welfare recipients, low literacy does not cause poverty, although it may restrict the ability to take advantage of opportunity. Nor will higher levels of literacy necessarily reduce poverty. Indeed, masses of well-educated, but underemployed, people are and historically have been flashpoints for social unrest, if not revolution. In our nation, with high levels of unemployment in the urban centers and a growing disparity between the wealthy and the poor, it is naive to ignore the operation of the social system and proceed as if literacy alone were the solution to poverty and educational underachievement. What is important is the availability of social and economic opportunity as a route out of poverty. In the entry-level labor market of today, applicants far outnumber jobs and few positions pay an adequate living wage or offer opportunities for advancement. The few good jobs for workers with little education or skills have been known to attract over 100 applicants for each position (D'Amico, 1997). Although one may applaud the work ethic and view the development of an organized lifestyle as preparation for economic opportunity should one be able to find it, the truth remains that the focus of public policy is on reducing the welfare rolls regardless of whether the work available will pay enough to lift people out of poverty or lead to future opportunity. As advocated by D'Amico and others concerned with the effects of the new welfare provisions, national policies of affordable child care and job creation to repair the nation's infrastructure are needed to help open up opportunities for both literacy learning and economic advancement.

At present, changes in skills, attitudes, and knowledge are required of individuals, with less pressure on employers to accommodate to the particular needs of these potential new workers. Public policy with respect to the needs of welfare recipients varies from state to state, and no national policy initiative to expand economic opportunity for former welfare clients is discernible. As with family literacy in previous years, the locus of change is the individual rather than or despite the social system. In the 1960s, social interventions were linked to social welfare and issues of equity. Today the linkage is to economic concerns, privatization, and global competition.

FAMILY LITERACY IN THE NEW POLITICAL CLIMATE

Even before enactment of the new welfare regulations, job readiness skills have been features of some family literacy and Even Start programs, and learners often came to programs because the prospect of a high school equivalence diploma held the promise of employability. Family literacy programs themselves have been viewed as first steps en route to additional education or job training programs that could lead to economic self-sufficiency. Personal qualities noted as outcomes of many programs, such as increased self-confidence, motivation, and goal direction, have clear importance for employment as for other life situations. Similarly, the skills of time management and household organization included in some parenting components of family literacy programs have been seen as useful to obtaining and holding jobs.

The restriction of welfare benefits to specified periods of time demand that these often implicit functions of family literacy programs be cast as prominent features. Because time for education is limited, family literacy programs may no longer function as an initial step, but as the first and only opportunity for education and job preparation. Alternatively, welfare recipients might choose community service work or training programs that closely link literacy and work skills, rather than a family literacy program. Some participants in quality Even Start programs have found employment or reduced their welfare benefits after leaving the program, but the spiral of improvement needed by others who reported continued enrollment in education or training programs may be cut short by the restriction on welfare benefits and the work mandate (Hayes, 1996).

The National Center for Family Literacy has responded to the changed legislation by incorporating more job-related skills into its programs and advocating family literacy as a strategy for welfare reform (Hayes, 1996). Most immediately, it has advocated the inclusion of schools as work sites for welfare recipients, enabling them to reap the benefits of parent involvement in the school and enhancement of literacy learning while fulfilling the mandated work requirement. As of fall 1998, no state had permitted this desirable change. The NCFL maintains that full-scale, high-intensity programs such as its Kenan model, can integrate job skills training into their program and thereby support the goals of welfare-to-work programs. Changes in instructional content were proposed so that "every component of family literacy programs, from adult education and parenting to parents and children together time will . . . focus on skills preparation." The workplace would be made a large part of the curriculum. In addition to their being direct preparation for work, the NCFL maintained, the maturity-enhancing activities of the Kenan model's parenting component and the parent-child relationships resulting from joint activities would strengthen participants so they could withstand stresses brought on by change, such as working in a job.

Three experimental welfare-to-work family literacy programs are described as incorporating various amounts of work experience, employment skills including basic literacy, and preschool education for the children. Night classes are provided for parents who must meet work requirements during the day. These complex programs require full-time commitment on the part of participants for 6 months to one year; they involve collaboration with many community partners and the blending of several funding streams.

In its 1997 publication, the National Center for Family Literacy suggests that Even Start and other large programs with experience in working with community partners are well positioned to collaborate with new ones, such as welfare agencies and employers. The Center advises family literacy programs to be more flexible about hours of service in order to provide evening hours for working parents and extended child care for preschoolers. It also urges the family literacy community to exert influence on emerging provisions of state welfare plans, advocating particularly that basic skills taught in job contexts be included in a state's definition of approved work activities.

As part of its proactive stance, the NCFL offers training on the challenges of welfare reform and family literacy and has embarked on a series of projects. Its Family Independence Initiative will develop and evaluate new models at 10 sites that are offering intensive family literacy services and attempting to move families from welfare to work (National Center for Family Literacy, 1998). As the name suggests, the focus is on literacy as a tool for economic advancement. In South Carolina, NCFL teams are working with local practitioners at several sites to redesign programs toward a focus on workplace content. Articulation of instruction with specific job opportunities is a feature of this effort; based on a survey of employment needs particular to a locality, customized learning packets are being designed for the family literacy sites in different parts of the state. Several models of work site experience are being used, including adult education at the work site, job shadowing, coaching, nontraditional job training for women, and work experience for those who are job ready before they have received a general equivalency diploma. Also in South Carolina, the NCFL has been using existing family literacy programs as work experience sites (Freeman, personal communication, 1997).

As family literacy programming changes and adapts to the external demand for workplace training, it is pertinent to ask what might be eliminated. Adult learners want opportunities to develop in their multiple life roles, as family members, workers, and citizens. Large programs may be able to incorporate all areas successfully and to devise curricula that integrate literacy learning into each. Small programs may not. Will there be opportunity to investigate racism, violence, and other societal factors that restrict life chances, and take action to combat them? Citizenship education, cultural exchange, parenting, and health and nutrition curricula may all be curtailed because of the focus on work for that large percentage of family literacy participants who are presently on welfare. With the mandate to move people off welfare, what will happen to parent-child interaction in family literacy programs? Will there be time for participants to learn about child development, books for children, and how to support children's reading and writing through interactive discussion and dialogue at home? Competing priorities have often emerged in family literacy programs. Under the press of welfare regulations, adults may want to concentrate on job preparation; they might not want to participate in the program's parent-child or parenting activities and time with children might seem distinctly secondary.

With the exception of Even Start, the effect on school-based programs is difficult to predict at this early stage of welfare reform. Work requirements and the need for workplace preparation are probably obstacles to participation by single parents and the welfare population. It seems doubtful that schools can meet those needs, particularly in the case of smaller programs.

Although all schools need and want family involvement, the resources that adult family and community members can bring to schools are especially salient to the success of education in high poverty areas. There, where academic achievement may be at risk, the support that children receive from home and school both working together on their behalf is especially needed. Of necessity, the workforce mandate of welfare reform drains that resource. It is unrealistic to expect parents of limited means, whether coming from single- or two-parent households, to fulfill 30 hours of work per week, deal with child care, their households, and the many exigencies of poverty and still maintain heavy involvement in the school. It is unlikely that a woman such as Ms. Smiley or Ms. Green could have participated in Family Reading regularly and put in many hours as a school volunteer under those circumstances. Not only will scheduled events such as Family Reading workshops be more difficult to sustain, the work demands of the new welfare regulations will make more difficult the kind of casual regular contact with the school that we have seen in the case of the mothers we have studied. Suburban schools unable to rely on volunteers from families in which parents work outside the home have established foundations to provide funds that once were raised by volunteers; many also open schools in the evenings to accommodate parents' schedules, or have instituted computer communications. Few inner-city schools are so equipped. The irony is that in order to maximize chances of not repeating the cycle of poverty and undereducation in the following generation, family involvement is needed. Thus the welfare changes, while leading to some possible increase in income and decrease in pressure on the public purse, may result in difficulties in the generation to come.

The more hopeful sign is that structures are in place for maintaining school-based family literacy programs. The importance of building partnerships with families is widely recognized in the education community. The federal initiative, Goals 2000, the Improving America's Schools Act, encourages home-school-community partnerships through a program of outreach and funding; as it is implemented on state and local levels, many schools are expanding parent services and developing workshops on school subjects, home visitations, and parent centers in schools, all of which could include family literacy as one of the services. The Elementary and Secondary Education Act specifies that a percentage of its funding be used for parent involvement. Also in recognition of the intergenerational influences on learning, as of July 1998, the national America Reads Challenge authorized funding for family literacy tutoring in addition to tutoring help for children.

Although there is no estimate of the number of smaller, school-based family literacy programs, national statistics provide some notion of an infrastructure that may accommodate family literacy programs. More than 80% of public elementary schools provide information to parents on topics ranging from homework help to parenting skills and child development; although the extent of their communication is not reported, 75% provide such information in workshops or classes. Also interesting as a site for family literacy activities are parent resource centers, a place in the school where parents can gather informally and get information on parenting and school-related issues; 47% of public elementary school have or are developing such a facility (National Center for Education Statistics, 1997).

Schools are likely to benefit also from the increasing attention to family literacy on the part of state and national policymakers. According to the National Institute for Literacy (1999), 13 states have enacted family literacy legislation and/or funding; in addition, federal funding for family literacy has increased tenfold over the past ten years. Significantly, in 1998 Congress mandated or strengthened mandates for family literacy in four important pieces of legislation, the Reading Excellence Act, the Workforce Investment Act (part of the Adult Education Act), the Even Start Family Literacy program, and the Head Start Act. Congress also formulated a consistent definition of family literacy to govern implementation of the four federal laws. As defined in those laws, family literacy services are to be sufficiently intense to make "sustainable changes in a family" and must include and integrate all of the following: "interactive literacy activities between parents and their children; training for parents . . . to be the primary teachers for their children and full partners in the education of their children; parent literacy training that leads to economic self-sufficiency; and an age-appropriate education to prepare children for success in school and life experiences" (National Institute for Literacy, 1999, p. 3). This mandate for intense, results-oriented, and comprehensive family literacy services will require educators receiving federal funding under these acts to meet the pressures of coordinating the varied components of a complex program and collaborating with many agencies.

The goal of family literacy programs is to replace the intergenerational cycle of low literacy and poverty with one of achievement and self-sufficiency. One means of advancing that goal is through helping both generations improve their literacy and helping parents support their children's social and academic development. School-based programs will most likely continue to serve adults and children at various levels of literacy. What is problematic is the degree to which they will reach former welfare clients—

those who would benefit from a nonthreatening reentry into the literacy arena, or those who wish to help their children, but do not yet know how. The challenge is to keep an even focus on the purposes of family literacy programs. In the current climate, programs are in danger of being driven by the exigencies of welfare reform.

In her essay on the meanings of literacy, Sylvia Scribner (1988) advances three metaphors. She says that literacy may be thought of as adaptation, a meaning that focuses on its pragmatic, functional value, as in the case of the adaptation of family literacy programs to the necessities of welfare reform. Literacy may also be thought of as power, a means of group or community advancement. Certainly in our society those who are literate have power and use literacy for purposes of power; low literacy is concentrated among the poor and minority populations, who are relatively powerless. Scribner questions, however, whether literacy can be the primary force for social change; Cochran (1987), discussing the empowerment process as one that helps individuals and groups in their efforts to achieve social equality, points out that limits are "imposed by the structural forces in the larger society" (p. 119). Implicit in the ethos of the family literacy movement is the concept of literacy as individual empowerment, the ability to take charge of one's life and influence events. The limitations of empowerment and the possibilities of group exercise of power remain to be explored.

Scribner's (1988) third metaphor is literacy as a state of grace. By that is meant a particular status of the literate person, a condition of enhancement of the self that involves intellectual, aesthetic, and spiritual participation in the accumulated creations and knowledge of humankind. Does this happen in family literacy programs? We see it in learners' faces as they read and discuss literature with one another or share books with their children.

Scribner's (1988) three metaphors are noncompeting. There should be room for each in family literacy programs. Do these multiple meanings of literacy matter? I suggest that they do, and in ways that are more than theoretical. Here is a recent example.

Two of my graduate students are conducting a family literacy program based on the Family Reading workshop model. After the second workshop, they told me about Jacques, father of a 2-year-old son. At their suggestion, he had borrowed a book to read to his child. In words that had been spoken many times over by program participants in the past, although usually by women, this father had said, "My son liked the book and I liked reading to him. I had been growing apart from my son. Reading to him brought us closer."

The deep enjoyment and human gratification of reading that energizes intrinsic motivation and sustains engagement must be a part of any family literacy effort no less than must the goal of literacy improvement. Individual and personal though such goals and gratifications may be, they nonetheless are significant to the broadest purposes of education. In *Democracy in America*, Tocqueville (1835/1945) made the connection: "The instruction of the people powerfully contributes to the support of the democratic republic; and such must always be the case . . . where the instruction which enlightens the understanding is not separated from the moral education which amends the heart" (p. 317). The example of Jacques and others like him resounds in a public world.

References

Afflebach, P. P., & Johnson, P. H. (1986). What do expert readers do when the main idea is not explicit? In J. Baumann (Ed.), *Teaching main idea comprehension.* Newark, DE: International Reading Association.

Allexhalt-Snider, M. (1995). Teachers' perspectives on their work with families in a bilingual community. *Journal of Research in Childhood Education, 9,* 85–95.

Anderson, R. C., Hiebert, E. H., Scott, J. A., & Wilkinson, I. A. G. (1985). *Becoming a nation of readers: The report of the Commission on Reading.* Washington, DC: National Institute of Education.

Auerbach, E. R. (1989). Toward a social-contextual approach to family literacy. *Harvard Educational Review, 59*(2), 165–181.

Auerbach, E. R. (1995). Deconstructing the discourse of strengths in family literacy. *Journal of Reading Behavior, 27*(4), 643–661.

Baker, L., Serpell, R., & Sonnenschein, S. (1995). Opportunities for literacy learning in the homes of urban preschoolers. In L. M. Morrow (Ed.), *Family Literacy: Connections in schools and communities* (pp. 236–252). Newark, DE: International Reading Association.

Barbara Bush Foundation for Family Literacy. (1989). *First teachers: A family literacy handbook for parents, policy-makers, and literacy providers.* Washington, DC: Barbara Bush Foundation for Family Literacy.

Bermudez, A., & Padron, Y. (1987). Integrating parental education into teacher training programs: A workable model for minority parents. *Journal of Educational Equity and Leadership, 7,* 235–244.

Bloem, P. L., & Padak, N. D. (1996). Picture books, young adult books, and adult literacy learners. *Journal of Adolescent & Adult Literacy, 40,* 48–53.

Bogdan, R., & Taylor, S. J. (1975). *Introduction to qualitative research methods: A phenomenological approach to the social sciences.* New York: John Wiley.

Bronfenbrenner, U. (1979). *The ecology of human development.* Cambridge, MA: Harvard University Press.

Cairney, T. H. (1995). Developing parent partnerships in secondary literacy learning. *Journal of Reading, 38,* 520–526.

Cairney, T. H., & Ruge, J. (1996, April). *Examining the impact of cultural mismatches between home and school: Coping with diversity in classrooms.* Paper presented at the conference of the American Educational Research Association, New York.

Chavkin, N., & Williams, D. (1988). Critical issues in teacher training for parent involvement. *Educational Horizons, 66,* 87–89.

Chrispeels, J. H. (1996, Nov.). Evaluating teachers' relationships with families: A case study of one district. *Elementary School Journal, 97,* 179–198.

Clark, R. M. (1983). *Family life and school achievement: Why poor black children succeed or fail.* Chicago: University of Chicago Press.

Cochran, M. (1987). Empowering families: An alternative to the deficit model. In K. Hurrelman, F. Kaufmann, & F. Losel (Eds.), *Social intervention: Policy and constraints* (pp. 105–120). New York: DeGruyter.

Coleman, J. S., Campbell, E. Q., Hobson, C. J., McPartland, J., Mood, A. M., Weinfeld, F. D., & York, R. L. (1966). *Equality of educational opportunity.* Washington, DC: U.S. Government Printing Office.

Comer, J. P. (1988). Educating poor minority children. *Scientific American, 259,* 42–48.

Connors, L. J. (1994). *Small wins: The promises and challenges of family literacy.* Baltimore: Center on Families, Communities, Schools, and Children's Learning, Johns Hopkins University.

Csikszentmihalyi, M. (1990). Literacy and intrinsic motivation. *Daedalus, 119,* 115–140.

Cuban, S., & Hayes, E. (1996). Women in family literacy programs: A gendered perspective. In P. Sissel (Ed.), *A community-based approach to literacy programs: Taking learners' lives into account* (pp. 5–16). San Francisco: Jossey-Bass.

D'Amico, D. (1997). *Adult education and welfare to work initiatives: A review of research, practice, and policy.* Report prepared under the fellowship program of the National Institute for Literacy, Washington, DC.

DeBruin-Parecki, A., Paris, S. G., & Siedenburg, J. (1997). Family literacy: Examining practice and issues of effectiveness. *Journal of Adolescent and Adult Literacy, 40,* 596–605.

Delgado-Gaitan, C. (1990). *Literacy for empowerment.* New York: Falmer Press.

Delgado-Gaitan, C. (1992). School matters in the Mexican American home: Socializing children to education. *American Educational Research Journal, 29,* 495–513.

Delpit, L. (1995). *Other people's children.* New York: New Press.

Durkin, D. (1966). *Children who read early.* New York: Teachers College Press.

Edwards, P. (1994). Responses of teachers and African-American mothers to a book-reading intervention program. In D. Dickinson (Ed.), *Bridges to literacy: Children, families, and schools* (pp. 175–208). Cambridge, MA: Blackwell.

Edwards, P. E. (1995). Combining parents' and teachers' thoughts about storybook reading at home and school. In L. M. Morrow (Ed.), *Family literacy: Connections in schools and communities* (pp. 54–69). Newark, DE: International Reading Association.

Enz, B. J., & Searfoss, L. W. (1995). Let the circle be unbroken: Teens as literacy learners and teachers. In L. M. Morrow (Ed.), *Family literacy: Connections in schools and communities* (pp. 115–128). Newark, DE: International Reading Association.

Epstein, J. L. (1987). Toward a theory of family-school connections: Teacher practices and parent involvement. In K. Hurrelman, F. Kaufmann, & F. Losel (Eds.), *Social intervention: Policy and constraints* (pp. 121–136). New York: DeGruyter.

Epstein, J. L. (1991). Effects of teacher practices of parent involvement on student achievement in reading and math. In S. Silvern (Ed.), *Advances in reading/ language research: Vol 5. Literacy through family, community, and school interaction.* Greenwich, CT: JAI Press.

Epstein, J. L. (1995, May). School/family/community partnerships: Caring for the children we share. *Phi Delta Kappan, 76,* 701–712.

Epstein, J. L., & Becker, H. J. (1982). Teacher practices of parent involvement: Problems and possibilities. *Elementary School Journal, 83,* 103–113.

Epstein, J. L., Clark, L., Salinas, K. C., & Sanders, M. (1997, March). *Scaling up school-family-community connections in Baltimore: Effects on student attendance and achievement.* Paper presented at the annual meeting of the American Educational Research Association, Chicago.

Epstein, J. L., & Dauber, S. (1991). School programs and teacher practices of parent involvement in inner-city elementary and middle schools. *Elementary School Journal, 91,* 289–303.

Erickson, F. (1986). Qualitative methods in research on teaching. In M. C. Wittrock (Ed.), *Handbook of research on teaching* (3rd ed.) (pp. 119–161). New York: Macmillan.

Evans-Schilling, D. (1996). Preparing educators for family involvement: Reflections, research, and renewal. *Forum of Education, 51,* 1.

Federal Interagency Forum on Child & Family Statistics. (1997). *America's children: Key national indicators of well being.* http://www.cdc.gov/nchswww/ about/otheract/children/child.htm

Finders, M., & Lewis, C. (1994). Why some parents don't come to school. *Educational Leadership, 51,* 50–54.

Foertsch, M. A. (1992). *Reading in and out of school: Factors influencing the literacy achievement of American students in grades 4, 8, and 12, in 1988 and 1990.* Washington, DC: Office of Educational Research and Improvement, U.S. Department of Education.

Ford Foundation. (1988). *Toward a More Perfect Union.* New York: Ford Foundation.

Freire, P., & Macedo, D. P. (1987). Literacy: Reading the word and the world. Westport, CT: Greenwood.

Gadsden, V. L. (1994). Understanding family literacy: Conceptual issues facing the field. *Teachers College Record, 96*(1), 58–86.

Gadsden, V. L., & Smith, R. R. (1994, Fall). African-American males and fatherhood: Issues in research and practice. *Journal of Negro Education, 63*(4), 634–648.

Garner, R. (1987). *Metacognition and reading comprehension.* Norwood, NJ: Ablex.

Genisio, M. H. (1996). Breaking barriers with books: A fathers' book-sharing program from prison. *Journal of Adolescent and Adult Literacy, 40,* 92–100.

Goldenberg, C., Reese, L., & Gallimore, R. (1992). Effects of literacy materials from school on Latino children's home experiences and early reading achievement. *American Journal of Education, 100,* 497–537.

Goldsmith, E. (1995). Deepening the conversation. *Journal of Reading, 38,* 558–563.

Goldsmith, E., & Handel, R. D. (1990). *Family reading: An intergenerational approach to literacy.* Syracuse, NY: New Readers Press.

Gowen, S. G., & Bartlett, C. (1997). "Friends in the kitchen": Lessons from survivors. In Glynda Hull (Ed.), *Changing work, changing workers: Critical perspectives on language, literacy, and skills* (pp. 141–158). Albany: State University of New York Press.

Griffin, G. A., Lieberman A., & Noto, J. J. (1982). *Interactive research and development on schooling: Final report of the implementation of the strategy.* New York: Teachers College, Columbia University.

Handel, R. D. (1990a). *The Partnership for Family Reading: Guide to replication.* Upper Montclair, NJ: Montclair State University.

Handel, R. D. (1990b, April). *Shared visions, double vision, and changing perspectives: A college/school parent participation program.* Paper presented at the annual meeting of the American Educational Research Association, Boston.

Handel, R. D. (1992). The partnership for family reading: Benefits for families and schools. *The Reading Teacher, 46,* 116–226.

Handel, R. D. (1995). Family reading at the middle school. *Journal of Reading, 38,* 528–540.

Handel, R. D., & Goldsmith, E. (1988). Intergenerational reading: A community college program. *Journal of Reading, 32,* 250–256.

Handel, R. D., & Goldsmith, E. (1989). Children's literature and adult literacy. Empowerment through intergenerational learning. *Lifelong Learning, 12,* 24–27.

Handel, R. D., & Goldsmith, E. (1994). Family reading—still got it: Adults as learners, literacy resources, and actors in the world. In D. Dickinson (Ed.), *Bridges to literacy: Children, families, and schools.* Cambridge, MA: Blackwell.

Hannon, P. (1995). *Literacy, home, and school: Research and practice in teaching literacy with parents.* London: Falmer Press.

Harding, S. (1991). *Whose science? Whose knowledge? Thinking from women's lives.* Ithaca: Cornell University Press.

Harris, T. L., & Hodges, R. E. (Eds.). (1995). *The literacy dictionary.* Newark, DE: International Reading Association.

Harry, B. (1996). Family literacy programs: Creating a fit with families of children with disabilities. In L. A. Benjamin & J. Lord (Eds.), *Family literacy: Direction in research and implications for practice* (pp. 34–49). Washington, DC: U.S. Department of Education, Office of Educational Research and Improvement.

Hayes, A. (1996). Family literacy as a strategy in welfare reform. *Window on the world of family literacy, 2,* 11–15.

Headman, R. (1993). Parents and teachers as co-investigators. In M. Cochran-Smith & S. L. Lytle (Eds.), *Inside outside: Teacher research and knowledge*. New York: Teachers College Press.

Heath, S. B. (1983). *Ways with words: Language, life, and work in communities and classrooms*. New York: Cambridge University Press.

Heath, S. B. (1995, December). *Reading, writing, and childhood: A look back to beginnings*. Address to the annual meeting of the National Reading Conference, New Orleans.

Henderson, A. T., & Berla, N. (Eds.). (1994). *A new generation of evidence: The family is critical to student achievement*. Columbia, MD: National Committee for Citizens in Education.

Herrmann, B. A., & Sarracino, J. (1991, April). *Student literacy through parent involvement*. Paper presented at the annual meeting of the American Educational Research Association, Chicago.

Hiebert, E. H. (Ed.). (1991). *Literacy for a diverse society: Perspectives, practices, and policies*. New York: Teachers College Press.

Hoover-Dempsey, K. V., & Sandler, H. M. (1997). Why do parents become involved in their children's education? *Review of Educational Research, 67*, 3–42.

Huey, E. B. (1908). *The psychology and pedagogy of reading*. New York: Macmillan.

Kazemek, F. (1988). Women and adult literacy: Considering the other half of the house. *Lifelong Learning, 11*, 15, 23–24.

Kirsch, I., & Jungeblut, A. (1986). *Literacy: Profiles of America's young adults*. Washington, DC: National Assessment of Educational Progress.

Krol-Sinclair, B. (1996a). Connecting home and school literacies: Immigrant parents with limited formal education as classroom storybook readers. In D. J. Leu, C. K. Kinzer, & K. A. Hinchman (Eds.), *Literacies for the 21st century: Research and practice* (pp. 270–283), 45th Yearbook of the National Reading Conference. Chicago: National Reading Conference.

Lareau, A. (1989). *Home advantage*. New York: Falmer Press.

Laster, B. P. (1996). From white elephant to cutting edge: The transformation of the reading clinic? In D. J. Leu, C. K. Kinzer, & K. A. Hinchman (Eds.), *Literacies for the 21st century: Research and practice* (pp. 408–419), 45th Yearbook of the National Reading Conference. Chicago: National Reading Conference.

Leichter, H. J. (1984). Families as environments for literacy. In H. Goelman, A. Oberg, & F. Smith (Eds.), *Awakening to literacy* (pp. 38–50). Portsmouth, NH: Heinemann.

Levenson, A. R., Reardon, E., & Schmidt, S. R. (1997). *The impact of welfare reform on AFDC recipients in Los Angeles County: Limited skills mean limited employment opportunities*. Santa Monica, CA: Milken Institute.

Levine, J. A., & Pitt, E. W. (1996). What's behind the fatherhood debate? A guide for family support practitioners. *Fatherhood and Family Support Report, 15* (pp. 4–5). Chicago: Family Resource Coalition.

Lightfoot, S. L. (1978). *Worlds Apart*. New York: Basic Books.

Lincoln, Y. S., & Guba, E. (1985). *Naturalistic inquiry.* Beverly Hills, CA: Sage.

Luttrell, W. (1989). Working-class women's ways of knowing: Effects of gender, race, and class. *Sociology of Education, 62,* 33–46.

Lytle, S. L., Belzer, A., & Reumann, R. (1992). *Invitations to inquiry: Rethinking staff development in adult literacy education.* Philadelphia: National Center on Adult Literacy, University of Pennsylvania.

MacDonald, J. B. (1994). *Teaching and parenting: Effects of the dual role.* Lantham, MD: University Press of America.

McIvor, M. C. (Ed.). (1990). *Family literacy in action: A survey of successful programs.* Syracuse, NY: New Readers Press.

McKee, P. A., & Rhett, N. (1995). The Even Start Family Literacy program. In L. M. Morrow (Ed.), *Family literacy: Connections in schools and communities* (pp. 155–166). Newark, DE: International Reading Association.

McLaughlin, M. W. (1990). The Rand change agent study revisited: Macro perspectives and micro realities. *Educational Researcher, 19*(9), 11–16.

Moles, O. (1993). Collaboration between schools and disadvantaged parents: Obstacles and openings. In N. F. Chavkin (Ed.), *Families and schools in a pluralistic society* (pp. 1–49). Albany: State University of New York Press.

Moll, L. (1992). Bilingual classroom studies and community analysis: Some recent trends. *Educational Researcher, 21,* 20–24.

Monaghan, E. J. (1991). Family literacy in early 18th-century Boston: Cotton Mather and his children. *Reading Research Quarterly, 26,* 342–370.

Morrow, L. M. (Ed.). (1995). *Family Literacy: Connections in schools and communities.* Newark, DE: International Reading Association.

Morrow, L. M., & Paratore, J. (1993). Family literacy: Perspective and practices. *The Reading Teacher, 47*(3), 194–200.

Morrow, L. M., Tracey, D. H., & Maxwell, C. M. (Eds.). (1995). *A survey of family literacy in the United States.* Newark, DE: International Reading Association.

National Center for Children in Poverty. (1998). *Young child poverty in the United States: Wide variation and significant change.* New York: Columbia University School of Public Health.

National Center for Education Statistics. (1997). *Survey on family and school partnerships in public schools, K–8.* Washington, DC: U.S. Department of Education.

National Center for Health Statistics/NY Times. (1998, July 21). *In climb up the ladder, married blacks are choosing smaller families. The New York Times,* p. A10.

National Center for Family Literacy. (1998). *Update.* Louisville, KY: Author.

National Governors Association. (1998). *Promoting responsible fatherhood: An update.* http://www.nga.org/pubs/issuebriefs

National Institute for Literacy. (1999). *Strengthening family literacy: How states can increase funding and improve quality.* Washington, DC: Author.

Neuman, S. B., Celano, D., & Fischer, R. (1996). The children's literature hour: A social-constructivist approach to family literacy. *Journal of Literacy Research, 28,* 499–523.

Neuman, S. B., Hagedorn, T., Celano, D., & Daly, P. (1995). Toward a collaborative approach to parent involvement in early education: A study of teenage
mothers in an African-American community. *American Educational Research
Journal, 32,* 801–827.

Nickerson, R. S. (1992). On the intergenerational transfer of higher-order skills. In
T. G. Sticht, M. J. Beeler, & B. A. McDonald (Eds.), *The Intergenerational
Transfer of Cognitive Skills,* Vol II (pp. 159–171). Norwood, NJ: Ablex.

Nickse, R. S. (1990). *Family and intergenerational literacy programs: An up-date
of "the noises of literacy".* Columbus, OH: ERIC Clearinghouse on Adult,
Career, and Vocational Education. (ERIC Document Reproduction Service
No. ED IN 342).

Nickse, R. S., & Englander, N. (1985). At-risk parents: Collaborations for literacy.
Equity and Choice, 1, 11–18.

Nickse, R. S., Speicher, A. M., & Buchek, P. S. (1988). An intergenerational adult
literacy project: A family intervention/prevention model. *Journal of Reading,
31,* 634–642.

Ogbu, J. U. (1988). Literacy and schooling in subordinate cultures: The case of
Black Americans. In E. R. Kintgen, B. M. Kroll, & M. Rose (Eds.), *Perspec-
tives on literacy* (pp. 227–242). Carbondale, IL: Southern Illinois University
Press.

Ortiz, R. W. (1996). Fathers' contribution to children's early literacy development:
The relationship of marital role functions. *Journal of Educational Issues of
Language Minority Students, 16,* 131–148.

Paratore, J. R. (1995). Implementing an intergenerational literacy project: Lessons
learned. In L. M. Morrow (Ed.), *Family literacy: Connections in schools and
communities* (pp. 37–54). Newark, DE: International Reading Association.

Philiber, W. W., Spillman, R. E., & King, R. E. (1996). Consequences of family
literacy for adults and children: Some preliminary findings. *Journal of Adolescent & Adult Literacy, 39,* 558–565.

Potts, M. W., & Paull, S. (1995). A comprehensive approach to family-focused
services. In L. M. Morrow (Ed.), *Family literacy: Connections in schools and
communities* (pp. 167–183). Newark, DE: International Reading Association.

Puchner, L. D., & Hardman, J. (1996, Fall). Family literacy in a cultural context:
Southeast Asian immigrants in the United States. *NCAL Connections.* Philadelphia: National Center on Adult Literacy, University of Pennsylvania, 1–3.

Purcell-Gates, V. (1995). *Other people's words: The cycle of low literacy.* Cambridge, MA: Harvard University Press.

Radcliffe, B., Malone, M., & Nathan, J. (1994). *Training for parent partnership:
Much more should be done.* Minneapolis: University of Minnesota, Center for
School Change.

Reinharz, S. (1992). *Feminist methods in social research.* New York: Oxford University Press.

Roman, L. G., & Apple, M. W. (1990). Is naturalism a move away from positiv-
ism? Materialist and feminist approaches to subjectivity in ethnographic research. In E. W. Eisner & A. Peshkin (Eds.), *Qualitative inquiry in education:
The continuing debate* (pp. 38–73). New York: Teachers College Press.

Scott-Jones, D. (1992). Family and community interventions affecting the development of cognitive skills in children. In T. G. Sticht, M. J. Beeler, & B. A.
McDonald (Eds.), *The intergenerational transfer of cognitive skills* (vol 1, pp.
84–108). Norwood, NJ: Ablex.

Scott-Jones, D. (1993). Families as educators in a pluralistic society. In N. F. Chavkin (Ed.), *Families and schools in a pluralistic society.* (pp. 245–254). Albany:
State University of New York Press.

Scott-Jones, D. (1997). *Families of color and school performance: Conceptual and
methodological issues.* Paper delivered at the annual meeting of the American
Educational Research Association, Chicago.

Scribner, S. (1988). Literacy in three metaphors. In E. R. Kintgen, B. M. Kroll, &
M. Rose (Eds.), *Perspectives on literacy* (pp. 71–81). Carbondale, IL: Southern
Illinois University Press.

Shanahan, T., Mulhern, M., & Rodriguez-Brown, F. (1995). Project FLAME: Lessons learned from a family literacy program for linguistic minority families.
The Reading Teacher, 48, 586–593.

Shartrand, A., Kreider, H., & Erickson-Warfield, M. (1994). *Preparing teachers to
involve parents: A national survey of teacher education programs.* Cambridge,
MA: Harvard Family Research Project, Harvard Graduate School of Education.

Shartrand, A., Weiss, H. B., Kreider, H. M., & Lopez, M. E. (1997). *New skills
for new schools: Preparing teachers in family involvement.* Cambridge, MA:
Harvard Family Research Project, Harvard Graduate School of Education.

Snow, C. E., Barnes, W. S., Chandler, J., Goodman, I. F., & Hemphill, L. (1991).
Unfulfilled expectations: Home and school influences on literacy. Cambridge,
MA: Harvard University Press.

Snow, C., & Tabors, P. (1996). Intergenerational transfer of literacy. In L. A. Benjamin & J. Lord (Eds.), *Family literacy: Directions in research and implications for practice* (pp. 73–80). Washington, DC: U.S. Department of Education.

Solsken, J. W. (1993). *Literacy, gender, & work in families and schools.* Norwood,
NJ: Ablex.

Spradley, J. P. (1979). *The ethnographic interview.* New York: Rinehart & Win-
ston.

Stacey, J. (1994). Backward toward the postmodern family. In G. Handel & G.
G. Whitchurch (Eds.), *The psychosocial interior of the family* (4th ed.) (pp.
643–668). New York: Aldine De Gruyter.

St. Pierre, R. G., Swartz, J. P., Murray, S., & Deck, D. (1996). *Improving family
literacy: Findings from the national Even Start evaluation.* Cambridge, MA:
Abt Associates.

Stein, S. G. (1997). *Equipped for the future: A reform agenda for adult literacy and
lifelong learning.* Washington, DC: National Institute for Literacy.

Sticht, T. G. (1992). The intergenerational transfer of cognitive skills. In T. G.
Sticht, M. J. Beeler, & B. A. McDonald (Eds.), *The intergenerational transfer
of cognitive skills* (vol 1, pp. 1–9). Norwood, NJ: Ablex.

Strauss, A. L., & Corbin, J. (1990). *Basics of qualitative research.* Newbury Park,
CA: Sage.

Swap, S. M. (1993). *Developing home-school partnerships*. New York: Teachers College Press.

Taylor, D. (1983). *Family literacy: Young children learning to read and write.* Portsmouth, NH: Heinemann.

Taylor, D., & Dorsey-Gaines, C. (1988). *Growing up literate: Learning from inner-city families.* Portsmouth, NH: Heinemann.

Taylor, D., & Strickland, D. (1986). *Family storybook reading.* Portsmouth, NH: Heinemann.

Tikunoff, W., Ward, B. A., & Griffin, G. A. (1975). *Interactive research and development on teaching study: Final report.* San Francisco: Far West Regional Laboratory.

Tizard, J., Schofield, W. N., & Hewison, J. (1982). Collaboration between teachers and parents in assisting children's reading. *British Journal of Educational Psychology, 52,* 1–15.

Tocqueville, A. de. (1945). *Democracy in America.* New York: Knopf. (Original work published 1835)

U.S. Department of Education. (1994). *Strong families, strong schools: Building community partnerships for learning.* Washington, DC: U.S. Government Printing Office.

Vygotsky, L. S. (1978). *Mind in society: The development of higher psychological processes.* Cambridge, MA: Harvard University Press.

Weick, K. E. (1984). Small wins: Redefining the scale of social problems. *American Psychologist, 39,* 40–49.

Weinstein-Shr, G. (1990, April). *Literacy and second language learners: A family agenda.* Paper presented at the annual meeting of the American Educational Research Association, Boston.

Weiss, H. B., & Jacobs, F. H. (1988). *Evaluating Family Programs.* Hawthorne, NY: Aldine de Gruyter.

Wikelund, K. R. (1993). *Motivations for learning: Voices of women welfare reform participants.* Philadelphia: National Center for Adult Literacy, University of Pennsylvania.

Selected Children's Books

Readings most frequently used in the Partnership for Family Reading program include the following.

Browne, A. (1988). *I like books*. New York: Knopf.

Friedman, I. N. (1984). *How my parents learned to eat*. New York: Houghton Mifflin.

Garza, C. L. (1990). *Family pictures/Cuadros de familia*. San Francisco: Children's Book Press.

Hoban, T. (1984). *I walk and read*. New York: Greenwillow.

Hoffman, M. (1991). *Amazing Grace*. New York: Dial.

Johnson, A. (1989). *Tell me a story, Mama*. New York: Orchard Books.

McDermott, G. (1972). *Anansi the spider*. New York: Henry Holt.

McQueen, L. (1985). *The little red hen*. New York: Scholastic.

McQueen, L., & Lopez, E. R. (1985). *La gallina roja*. New York: Scholastic.

Morris, A. (1989). *Bread bread bread*. New York: Lothrop, Lee, & Shepard.

Oram, H. (1984). *In the attic*. New York: Henry Holt.

Patterson, F. (1985). *Koko's kitten*. New York: Scholastic.

Ringgold, F. (1991). *Tar Beach*. New York: Crown.

Rohmer, H. (1989). *Uncle Nacho's hat/El sombrero del tio Nacho*. San Francisco: Children's Book Press.

Schenk de Regniers, S., Moore, E., White, M. M., & Carr, J. (Eds.). (1988). *Sing a song of popcorn*. New York: Scholastic.

Stanek, M. (1989). *I speak English for my mom*. Niles, IL: Albert Whitman.

Steptoe, J. (1987). *Mufaro's beautiful daughters*. New York: Lothrop, Lee, & Shepard.

Steptoe, J. (1986). *Stevie*. New York: Harper.

Titherington, J. (1987). *A place for Ben*. New York: Greenwillow.

Turkel, B. (1976). *Deep in the forest*. New York: Dutton.

Van Allsburg, C. (1981). *Jumanji*. Boston: Houghton Mifflin.

Wang, M. L. (1986). *The lion and the mouse*. Chicago: Children's Press.

Wang, M. L., & Kratky, L. J. (1988). *El leon y el raton*. Chicago: Children's Press.

Williams, V. (1986). *A chair for my mother*. New York: Greenwillow.

Index

Tabors, P., 16, 17, 46, 50, 98
Take Up Reading Now, 22
Taylor, D., 7, 12, 98, 101, 125, 137
Taylor, S. J., 114
Teacher education programs, 2, 140, 141–
    42, 144
Teachers, 29, 30, 52
    adult relationships, 117–19
    assumptions about parents, 109, 133
    early reading memories of, 109–10, 111
    as family literacy educators, 130, 131
    as family literacy learners, 3, 106–19
    family lives of, 117
    and Family Reading workshops, 50, 55
    meaning of Partnership experience to,
        113–19, 131
    in Newark, 44
    perspectives of, 34–37, 54
    professional knowledge of, 74–75
    relations with parents, 134, 142, 143
    reward structure for, 143
    role as family educators, 30, 113
Teaching, gendered nature of, 121
Television, 78, 82, 85, 86, 88, 95
Test-taking skills, 114–15
Text, 50, 110
    relating personal experiences to, 45, 47, 48
Tikunoff, W., 108
Tizard, J., 18
Tocqueville, A. de, 155
Tracey, D. H., 22
Transformation, 103
Transportation, 35, 124, 147

U.S. Department of Education, 18, 32, 35
U.S. Office of Bilingual Education and Mi-
    nority Language Affairs, 21

Values, articulation with, 58, 116, 133
Vocabulary development, 50, 73
Volunteering in schools, 25–26, 87, 93,
    119, 152
Vygotsky, L. S., 11, 15, 46

Ward, B. A., 108
Weinstein-Shr, G., 7, 54
Weiss, H. B., 106, 131
Welfare, 145–46
Welfare policy, implications of, 146–49
Welfare reform, 3, 149–50, 151–54
    work mandates, 122, 139, 146–47, 150,
        151–52
Welfare-to-work family literacy programs,
    150, 151
Whites, 15
Whole language, 135
Wikelund, K. R., 54
Wilkinson, I. A. G., 7
Williams, D., 106
Williams, Vera B., 47–48
Women, 11
    commonalities among, 95–98
    participants in Partnership for Family
        Reading, 42, 53–62
    predominance of, 25, 122–23, 138
    role of literacy in lives of, 104
    and welfare reform, 147
Work mandates, 122, 139, 146–47, 150,
    151–52
Work obligations
    and participation, 93, 97
Work site experience models, 151
Workforce Investment Act, 153
Wright, Richard, 127
Writing, 9, 16, 97, 114, 115

About the Author

Ruth D. Handel is Associate Professor in the Department of Reading and Educational Media at Montclair State University, Upper Montclair, New Jersey. Her Ph.D. is from Columbia University. Dr. Handel, one of the early developers of the field of family literacy, has worked with families and teachers for the past fifteen years. Her early work was recognized as a pioneering program by the Barbara Bush Foundation for Family Literacy. She is co-author of the first published family literacy curriculum, *Family Reading: An Intergenerational Approach to Literacy*, and the author of articles and research studies. Dr. Handel consults to school districts, corporations, and community agencies.